Mackenzie Jervis

111 Places in Las Vegas That You Must Not Miss

Photographs by Kaitlyn Kelsey

emons:

To Stephen, for moving us to this crazy city and for your unwavering support.

Bibliographical information of the Deutsche Nationalbibliothek
The Deutsche Nationalbibliothek lists this publication in
the Deutsche Nationalbibliografie; detailed bibliographical data
are available on the internet at http://dnb.d-nb.de.

Cäcilienstraße 48, 50667 Köln
info@emons-verlag.de

Cover icon: AdobeStock/trekandphoto
© Photographs by Kaitlyn Kelsey, except Absinthe (ch. 1): Spiegelworld;
Gold Strike Hot Springs (ch. 40): Desert Adventures;
Mob Museum (ch. 62): The Mob Museum
Design: Anja Sauerland, based on a design
by Lübbeke | Naumann | Thoben
Maps: altancicek.design, www.altancicek.de
Editor: Tania Taylor
Printing and binding: sourc-e GmbH
Printed in Europe 2025
ISBN 978-3-7408-2467-9
First edition

Guidebooks for Locals & Experienced Travelers
Join us in uncovering new places around the world at
www.111places.com

Foreword

When I first moved to Las Vegas, I viewed it like many people: as a fun getaway to have great food, get a little crazy, and forget your daily life. But what about living there? A city built on superficial entertainment seemed an awful place to live. I pictured my 22-year-old self on my first, and only, visit: walking down the Strip with loud music, car horns blaring, and drunken antics at all hours of the day and night.

When the opportunity came to seek out 111 places in Las Vegas, I thought maybe I would be able to find a few cool things beyond the typical top-10 list and learn the history of my new home. Little did I know that I would gain an appreciation for the city and its people in a way I never knew I could. The tough, extravagant external façade of Las Vegas is just that: a façade. Beneath is a warm and caring city, dedicated to enriching those who live here. Each person I have met has shown an overwhelming pride in their city, well beyond anything I could have imagined.

Las Vegas is a city unlike any other in the world, with industry, gaming, and historic preservation almost on equal footing. Where else can you tour atomic testing sites in the morning, explore mid-century neighborhoods in the afternoon, and catch an awe-inspiring circus act or magic show by night? Las Vegas is deeper than the larger-than-life reputation it has. And while I've had the opportunity to live in many amazing places in the world, Las Vegas is one that will always stick with me.

It's a city shaped by dreamers, builders, and performers – from the neon artists in the Arts District to the family-run restaurants tucked into unassuming strip malls. There's a rhythm to life here that's as vibrant as it is resilient. I hope this book helps you see beyond the surface, and that, like me, you come to admire the city's quirky charm, rich history, and the community that thrives just beneath the glitter.

111 Places

1___ Absinthe
The local-favorite "farcical" circus show | 10

2___ Airmail Navigation Arrows
Remnants of the Transcontinental Airway System | 12

3___ Al Davis Memorial Torch
The torch at the heart of Raider Nation | 14

4___ Aloha Specialties
When you live in Paradise, you vacation in Vegas | 16

5___ Art-o-mat Vending Machines
Discover miniature art in vintage vending machines | 18

6___ Atomic Liquors
The first freestanding bar in Las Vegas | 20

7___ Atomic Museum
Explore Nevada's contribution to the Atomic Age | 22

8___ Berlin Wall Urinals
A chance to pee on a piece of Cold War history | 24

9___ The Beverly Theater
Vegas' only independent film house | 26

10___ Black Sacrament Tattoo
All-female shop with dark and nerdy vibes | 28

11___ Blacksmith Classes
Learn the old ways at the Old Fort | 30

12___ Blue Angel Sculpture
Iconic piece of downtown history finds a new home | 32

13___ Boulder Dam Hotel
Famed hotel of the Hoover Dam project | 34

14___ Broadacres Marketplace
Local flea market celebrating Latino culture | 36

15___ Bugsy Siegel Monument
Marker for the mobster who "invented" Las Vegas | 38

16___ Burlesque Hall of Fame
A dazzling homage to burlesque's rich legacy | 40

17___ Cactus Joe's Nursery
Beloved plant nursery dedicated to desert flora | 42

18___ Casino Quest
Learn to gamble from the pros, without the risk | 44

19___ Cemetery Pulp
Oddities shop for "the weird and nerdy" | 46

20___ Center for Brain Health
A deconstructivist building housing cognitive care | 48

21___ Charleston Peak Winery
Sip wine at Nevada's largest producer | 50

22___ Cliff's Barber Corral
Barber with an Old West flair | 52

23___ Coffinwood
Coffin-shaped oasis in the heart of the desert | 54

24___ Cold War National Memorial
Hidden heroes honored at Mount Charleston | 56

25___ Community Healing Garden
A serene spot for hope and reflection | 58

26___ Corn Creek Springs
Landmark railroad-tie home on the wildlife refuge | 60

27___ CSN Planetarium
View stars, shows, and NASA artifacts | 62

28___ Desert Princess Riverboat
Mississippi riverboat on Lake Mead | 64

29___ The Dinosaur House
Home overtaken by prehistoric paraphernalia | 66

30___ Discovery Children's Museum
A three-story journey of fun, learning, and wonder | 68

31___ Dulceria La Colmena
Latin American treats, piñatas, and goods | 70

32___ El Cortez Hotel and Casino
The longest-running casino in Las Vegas | 72

33___ Featherblade Craft Butchery
The city's only sustainable butcher shop | 74

34___ Fergusons Downtown
Shop local at a bygone motel #rootedin community | 76

35___ First Statue of Liberty
The city's original and lesser-known Lady Liberty | 78

36___ Four-Faced Brahma Shrine
The only Brahma shrine in the Western world | 80

37___ Gamblers General Store
Shop at the world's largest gambling supply shop | 82

38___ Garden Farms
Empowering locals to grow their own food | 84

39 Gipsy Nightclub
Club at the center of Vegas' queer history | 86

40 Gold Strike Hot Springs
The hot spring oasis near the Hoover Dam | 88

41 The Golden Tiki
An offbeat haunt in a Chinatown strip mall | 90

42 Grave of Yonema Tomiyasu
Resting place of pioneer horticulturist | 92

43 Harrison House
Visit a segregation-era guesthouse | 94

44 Helen J. Stewart Statue
Monument to the First Lady of Las Vegas | 96

45 High School Senior Squares
Student monument at the city's first high school | 98

46 Historic Railroad Trail
Hike to the Hoover Dam | 100

47 Historic Westside Legacy Park
Park dedicated to Black History and the Westside | 102

48 Hotel Apache
Fremont's famed haunted hotel | 104

49 Huntridge Theater
Legendary theater brought back to life | 106

50 Il Toro E La Capra
Mexican-Italian fusion | 108

51 International Theater at The Westgate
Elvis' most famous venue in Vegas | 110

52 Jean-Marie Auboine Chocolatier
High-end French chocolates with a twist | 112

53 Kaqun Wellness Spa
One-of-a-kind wellness experience | 114

54 Kiel Ranch
One of the earliest ranches in the valley | 116

55 Las Vegas Circus Center
Learn from Vegas' best performers | 118

56 The Las Vegas Farm
Sanctuary giving animals a second chance at life | 120

57 Las Vegas Mannequins
Free "museum" of shop mannequins | 122

58 Liberace Garage
Extravagant cars from the famed performer | 124

59___ Little Church of the West
Say "I do" at Elvis' Viva Las Vegas wedding chapel | 126

60___ Luv-It Frozen Custard
Hand-crafted frozen custard since 1973 | 128

61___ Mermaid Swimmers
Real mermaids in the middle of the desert | 130

62___ Mob Museum
Mafia courthouse turned organized-crime museum | 132

63___ Mondays Dark at The Space
Biweekly variety show for charity | 134

64___ Mt. Charleston CCC Sites
Explore the mountain cultivated in the 1930s | 136

65___ Nellis Dunes
View the entire valley from here | 138

66___ Nelson's Ghost Town
Abandoned land of lawlessness, greed, and murder | 140

67___ Neon Museum Las Vegas
Disused neon brought back to life | 142

68___ Nevada Veterans Memorial
Sculptures commemorating sacrifice and valor | 144

69___ Nuwu Art Gallery
POC-owned creative hub and gallery | 146

70___ Oddfellows
A nightclub for people who don't like nightclubs | 148

71___ Old Country Boots
Custom boots for cowboys or wannabes | 150

72___ One of Vegas' Oldest Houses
Houses built for the railroad still stand downtown | 152

73___ Original McCarran Entrance
Preserved entrance to Las Vegas' first airport | 154

74___ Pedal and Pour
Bike and coffee shop creating community in LV | 156

75___ Pinball Hall of Fame
Retro paradise on the Strip | 158

76___ Pioneer Saloon
Visit the oldest bar in Southern Nevada | 160

77___ Pole Fitness Studio
Fitness classes fit for Las Vegas | 162

78___ The Punk Rock Museum
Play your favorite punk rocker's guitar | 164

79 Radial Symmetry
Giant sculpture honoring Paiute craftsmanship | 166

80 Rat Pack Footprints
Walk in the footsteps of legendary entertainers | 168

81 ReBAR
Where everything is for sale, even your seat | 170

82 Saginaw's Shrimp Cocktail
Try the recipe that made this dish world-famous | 172

83 Sahara West Library
Free art gallery in a local library | 174

84 The Sand Dollar Lounge
Iconic dive bar with live music and killer cocktails | 176

85 The Scotch 80s
Unaltered mid-century modern neighborhood | 178

86 Seven Magic Mountains
Dayglow rock pillars in the Nevada desert | 180

87 Siegfried and Roy Estate
Former home of the famed illusionist duo | 182

88 Sigma Derby
Play the analog table game with its own Facebook page | 184

89 Silver State Horseback Riding Tours
Escape the city with calm horses on the trail | 186

90 The Simpson House
Beloved cartoon home in a Las Vegas suburb | 188

91 Skyfall Panoramic Bar & Lounge
Elegant bar with a surprising view | 190

92 Sloan Canyon Petroglyph Site
Hike to Archaic era petroglyphs | 192

93 Slot Car City
Nostalgic haven for slot car enthusiasts | 194

94 The Smelly Bar
Take home a whiff of your favorite Vegas resort | 196

95 Snappy's
Retro Americana in an ever-evolving city | 198

96 Springs Preserve's Nature Exchange
Kids share nature finds to earn exciting rewards | 200

97 St. Thomas Ghost Town
Abandoned town long submerged beneath Lake Mead | 202

98 Strip Benchmarks
Brass medallions on the legendary neon boulevard | 204

99___ The Tank Pool
Take a waterslide through a shark tank | 206

100___ Themed Street Names
Quirky addresses inspired by cartoon favorites | 208

101___ Tom Devlin's Monster Museum
Exhibits dedicated to horror movie magic | 210

102___ Tule Springs Ranch
Quickie weddings and quickie divorces | 212

103___ Underground Mansion
Enter a luxury Cold War-era subterranean home | 214

104___ Vegas Theatre Company
The playhouse at the heart of the Arts District | 216

105___ Velveteen Rabbit
Indulge in cocktails that redefine the experience | 218

106___ Vibes DIY Studio
Vegas' top do-it-yourself art studio | 220

107___ Viva Las VegaStamps!
Shop with the largest collection of rubber stamps | 222

108___ Votes for Women Historic Marker
Honoring Las Vegas' role in women's suffrage | 224

109___ Warsaw Ghetto Remembrance Garden
Pieces of Holocaust history in Las Vegas | 226

110___ Water Street District
Henderson's historic street, brought back to life | 228

111___ Wax Trax Records
Local record shop bursting at the seams | 230

1 Absinthe

The local-favorite "farcical" circus show

Las Vegas is known for its over-the-top entertainment, but few shows capture the city's wild spirit quite like *Absinthe*. One of the most thrilling, irreverent, and unforgettable productions on the Strip, *Absinthe* is presented by Spiegelworld, a company famous for its edgy, immersive, and often outrageous theatrical experiences. Captivating audiences since 2011, it is performed inside a vintage European-style "spiegeltent" just outside Caesars Palace, creating an intimate setting where every seat feels like the front row.

Spiegelworld, founded by Ross Mollison, is all about pushing boundaries. With a mission to blend circus, burlesque, and variety theater with a provocative modern twist, the company has made *Absinthe* its flagship production. The show has become a must-see for visitors wanting a uniquely Vegas experience that's as wild as it is jaw-dropping. But what's more, it's a standout favorite among locals, a tough spot to secure when there are virtually unlimited shows to enjoy every day of the week.

Absinthe mixes cirque-style acrobatics, vaudeville comedy, and burlesque, delivered with plenty of adult humor. When asked why he thought the show was such a hit, Mollison said, "It's just something where, with entertainment, sometimes you hit the moment, the right vibe at the right time." With its raw energy, intimate venue, and no-rules atmosphere, it's everything you expect from a Vegas show. And so much more.

And while the gasp-worthy moments continue for multiple shows each night, the performance is ever changing, which may be one reason it's such a crowd favorite, especially among locals. "It's always growing. If you go to *Absinthe* tonight you're going to see a whole lot of new ideas," Mollison told the *Las Vegas Review-Journal* after the show's 14th anniversary. "We have an expression: 'Stand still and rot.' We are not standing still."

Address 3570 Las Vegas Boulevard South, Las Vegas, NV 89109, +1 (702) 534-3419, www.spiegelworld.com/shows/absinthe, boxoffice@spiegelworld.com | Getting there Deuce on the Strip Bus to Caesars Palace Hotel & Casino | Hours Shows Sun–Thu 8pm & 10pm, Fri & Sat 7pm, 9pm & 11pm | Tip Try out another one of Spiegelworld's shows, the *Atomic Saloon Show* at The Venetian (3377 Las Vegas Boulevard South, www.spiegelworld.com/shows/atomic-saloon-show).

2 Airmail Navigation Arrows

Remnants of the Transcontinental Airway System

Domestic US Air Mail was established on May 15, 1918, ushering in a new age of communication. During this era in aviation, pilots relied on geographical markers as radio navigation wouldn't become reliable until the '30s or '40s. To make night flying possible, a series of navigational beacons were constructed across the country, spaced about 25 miles apart, to act as markers for the transcontinental flights. The beacons had large 50- to 70-foot concrete arrows on the ground with accompanying lights to illuminate them. The first night airmail flights occurred in July 1924, eliminating the need to transfer mail to rail cars at night, and drastically decreasing delivery time for coast-to-coast airmail. By 1933, over 1,500 beacons were constructed, covering over 18,000 miles.

While the main Transcontinental system went from New York City to San Francisco, a southern branch ran from Salt Lake City to Los Angeles, crossing over Las Vegas, much like the railroad not long before. These beacons didn't last long, however. Many were removed during WWII to prevent aiding enemy bombers. But many arrows still remain today, becoming a draw for history and aviation enthusiasts across the country. Las Vegas and the surrounding desert region are lucky to have a few intact arrows from an often forgotten piece of history.

While a handful are scattered around the valley, one of the most accessible is in the town of Borax, just west of Jean along Las Vegas Boulevard. This was part of CAM (Contract Air Mail) Route 04, which ran from Salt Lake City to Los Angeles. The tower no longer remains, having been removed for scrap metal, but the arrow, a large concrete slab on the ground, is still in good shape despite baking in the sun for decades. This large arrow, smack in the middle of the desert, makes you appreciate the vastness of the country and how difficult it would have been to traverse over 100 years ago.

Address Las Vegas Boulevard South, Borax, NV 89019 | Getting there By car, take I-15 S to exit 12 at Jean. Take Las Vegas Boulevard South after 3.5 miles to the arrow on the left-hand side | Hours Unrestricted | Tip For a more exciting aviation experience, head to Sky Combat Ace to fly in a real stunt plane with a USAF veteran fighter pilot (2634 Airport Drive #106, North Las Vegas).

3 Al Davis Memorial Torch

The torch at the heart of Raider Nation

While the Raiders football team may have spent the majority of their history elsewhere, the traditions and legacy of the organization are alive and well in Vegas. One larger-than-life tradition is the Al Davis Memorial Torch. Al Davis, the Raiders long-time owner, AFL Coach of the Year, AFL Commissioner, and Pro Football Hall of Fame inductee, is credited as the architect of the Raiders' Commitment to Excellence. The torch is in recognition of Mr. Davis' vision that "the fire that burns brightest in the Raiders' organization is the will to win," a motto etched into the side of the torch.

Since Davis' death in 2011, the Raiders have invited alumni, celebrities, and notable community figures to light the memorial torch in his honor before each home game. The original torch at the Oakland Coliseum was about eight feet tall and can still be found, flame constantly burning, outside the Raiders facilities in Henderson.

Since their move to Las Vegas in 2020, a new torch presides over the stadium. At 93 feet, the torch is the world's tallest free-standing 3D-printed object. Crafted by Dimensional Innovations, working closely with current owner Mark Davis (son of Al Davis), it is made of carbon fiber and reinforced polycarbonate composite while the flame is a mixture of lights and special effects. It took 18 employees over 50,000 hours to develop, create, and install. CEO of Dimensional Innovations, Tucker Trotter, said, "The enormity of the torch, both physically and ideologically, will carry on the memory of Mr. Davis for years to come." Fittingly, the first person to light the new torch was his widow Carol Davis.

Thanks to its impressive size and glowing red and orange "flames," the torch is visible throughout the entire stadium, but for an up-close look at the torch and to experience ultra-exclusive areas such as the locker rooms, broadcast booth, and the field, take an Allegiant Stadium Tour.

Address 3333 Al Davis Way, Las Vegas, NV 89118, +1 (725) 780-3061, www.allegiantstadium.com/tours, tours@raiders.com | Getting there Deuce on the Strip Bus to Mandalay Bay | Hours Check website for tour schedule | Tip Continue on your Raiders-themed day with a stop at Raiders Tavern & Grill at the M Resort for themed decor and memorabilia (12300 Las Vegas Boulevard South, Henderson, www.themresort.com/dining/raiders-tavern-and-grill).

4 Aloha Specialties

When you live in Paradise, you vacation in Vegas

According to the US Census, Clark County has the highest population of native Hawaiians outside of Hawaii. In fact, there are so many Hawaiian people in Las Vegas that it's affectionately called the Ninth Island.

If there was a central guiding light to draw Hawaiians to Las Vegas, it's the California Hotel – or the Cal to locals – whose slogan is "Aloha spoken here." Opened in 1975 by Sam Boyd, it was the first property that would go on to become Boyd Gaming (owners of casinos like Main Street Station and Aliante Casino), which is now one of the largest casino-management companies in the country.

The Cal's original intended clientele was, you guessed it, gamblers from California. But only a year after opening, the casino struggled. William Boyd, Sam's son, wrote in the foreword of a 2007 book about the hotel, that his dad came to him and said, "We're going to need a niche market here and that's going to be Hawai'i."

Sam had developed a love for the islands and their people after several years of living and working in Honolulu. Sam also knew that most locals seemed to love gambling, which has always been illegal on the islands. With promotions like free rooms, discounted airfares on weekly chartered flights, and credits for a meal at a restaurant called Aloha Specialties, Hawaiian visitors began to flock to Vegas.

Aloha Specialties has been a staple at the Cal since. It's a no-frills diner, decorated in bright colors with island decor and family photos on the walls. It's typically packed around the clock with hungry travelers and locals alike to eat island favorites like Spam musubi, loco moco, mac salad, and teriyaki steak. One customer, a native of Hawaii, says his family has been coming to Vegas for over 20 years and they never miss a stop at the restaurant. Despite Hawaiian and Pacific Island food being a staple in most corners of Las Vegas, the appeal of Aloha Specialties isn't fading anytime soon.

Address 12 E Ogden Avenue #2F, Las Vegas, NV 89101, +1 (702) 382-1222, thecal.boydgaming.com | **Getting there** Deuce on the Strip Bus to Carson after Casino Center | **Hours** Sun–Wed 9am–7pm, Thu–Sat 9am–9pm | **Tip** For snacks and goods straight from Hawaii, make your way to Leilani's Attic (4749 S Maryland Parkway, www.leilanisattic.com).

5 Art-o-mat Vending Machines

Discover miniature art in vintage vending machines

The Cosmopolitan of Las Vegas' one-time tagline, "Just the Right Amount of Wrong," is unmistakable in the dimly lit and dark-hued lobby, where digital art, displayed on massive pillars, shows silhouettes of bodies moving seductively. But this isn't the only art showcased on the property. The Cosmopolitan has hundreds of contemporary artworks by both established and emerging artists from all over the world. Designed to inspire discovery, the collection includes large-scale paintings, photography, mixed-media works, sculptures, murals, and more.

Possibly the quirkiest pieces are the Art-o-mat vending machines. Created by Clark Whittington, these repurposed antique cigarette vending machines dispense art instead of cigarettes. The first Art-o-mat machine was featured in an art show in 1997 in Winston-Salem, North Carolina, and sold black-and-white Polaroids. His inspiration came from seeing a friend's need for a snack after hearing someone open a vending-machine snack.

Today, the mid-century modern-styled Art-o-mat machines can be found in museums and businesses around the US, but the largest collection is at The Cosmopolitan with a total of nine machines, with six in public areas such as the lobby, shopping areas, and casino floor. Whittington's personal favorite is the machine near The Chandelier because of its silver color set against the impressive, elegant chandelier.

Whittington's goal for the Art-o-mat machines is to provide easier access to art and create a connection between artists and buyers. The machines' unique appearance and strategic locations attract visitors who may otherwise never purchase art. Visitors can buy pieces like sketches, watercolor paintings, photographs, and small sculptures in specially designed boxes. The art is regularly swapped out, allowing for an endless source of small art for collectors and art lovers.

Address 3708 Las Vegas Boulevard South, Las Vegas, NV 89109, +1 (702) 698-7000, www.cosmopolitanlasvegas.com | Getting there Deuce on The Strip Bus to Bellagio/Cosmopolitan (Southbound) or Planet Hollywood (Northbound) | Hours Unrestricted | Tip Browse The Cosmo's art exhibits, such as *The Golden Age of Glam*, a collection of vintage photos promoting Las Vegas and its iconic sites, and performers like Tempest Storm, Liberace, Sinatra, and Elvis. Found on the Level 2 walkway between the Chelsea and Boulevard Towers.

6 Atomic Liquors

The first freestanding bar in Las Vegas

Just east of the Fremont Street Experience is Atomic Liquors, the first and longest-running freestanding bar in Las Vegas. The iconic neon sign out front promoting "Liquor and Cocktails" has been a staple of Fremont Street since the early '50s. Stella and Joe Sobchik opened Virginia's Café in 1945 after taking over Stella's mother's gas station and garage. Despite hardships from the war, the café did reasonably well, but Joe, tired of cooking, decided to open a liquor store called Atomic Liquors. When atomic testing began at the Nevada Test Site in 1951, many of its visitors would flock to the bar's roof to get a glimpse of the mushroom clouds.

Joe and Stella purchased a liquor "pouring" license, allowing Atomic Liquors to serve alcohol in the building alongside their take-out business and become the first freestanding bar in Las Vegas. Joe served them one of his specialty drinks, the Atomic Cocktail, a mix of vodka, brandy, and dry champagne. In 1952, the city established "The Tavern License," and Atomic Liquors was issued license #00001, which they still have today.

Many of the bar's patrons were working class, but celebrities like the Rat Pack, Barbra Streisand, and Clint Eastwood also visited, wishing to avoid attention on the Strip. An episode of *The Twilight Zone* called "The Gauntlet" was filmed inside, as well as parts of *The Hangover* and *Casino* (Martin Scorsese used the garage next door as a production studio).

In a city that's constantly changing, evolving, and trying to reinvent itself, Atomic Liquors has remained a constant, unchanging landmark in all the right ways. With some updates, such as the nuclear-themed cocktails like the Gamma Bay and Nevada Test Shot, its new kitchen next door, and some new decor to pay homage to the Sobchiks and the atomic age, visitors will love visiting this icon of Fremont Street.

Address 917 E Fremont Street, Las Vegas, NV 89101, +1 (702) 982-3000, www.atomic.vegas, info@atomic.vegas | **Getting there** Deuce on the Strip Bus to 4th at Fremont Street Experience | **Hours** Sun–Thu noon–2am, Fri & Sat noon–3am | **Tip** To continue your atomic-themed drinking, try out Able Baker Brewing Company, named after the first two atomic tests in Nevada, "Able" and "Baker," to learn about the legend of the Atomic Duck (1510 S Main Street, #120, www.ablebakerbrewing.com).

7 Atomic Museum

Explore Nevada's contribution to the Atomic Age

The Nevada Test Site (NTS), now called the Nevada National Security Site, is located north of Las Vegas on 1,350 square miles within a massive area of federally owned land. It was home to over 100 atmospheric and 828 underground tests between 1951 and 1992. The tests included infamous ones like Annie and Apple-2 in 1953 and 1955, respectively. These were detonated at "Doom Towns" inhabited by mannequins wearing clothes donated by JCPenney. Testing in Nevada was primarily done to assess different weapon designs and determine the impact of nuclear weapons on man-made structures and equipment.

Former workers started the Nevada Test Site Historical Foundation to ensure the site's history would not be forgotten. The NTSHF went on to open the Atomic Museum in 2005. Today, it's a Smithsonian affiliate that focuses mainly on Nevada's role in nuclear testing, but also all of America's nuclear history, starting at Los Alamos up until today.

The 10,000-square-foot museum walks you through the entire history of the Atomic Age and includes hundreds of authentic artifacts like the light from the top of the BREN Tower, which was used at the NTS in the 1960s to better understand the effects of radiation. A fan favorite is the Mark III bomb casing, which is the same type of device as the Fat Man bomb. View up close a substance created from the sand during the Trinity test in the New Mexico desert called Trinitite. Walk through the huge pipe-like Decoupler used in horizontal underground testing, or experience a simulated viewing of an atomic blast. The museum's artifacts from the atomic craze of the '50s and '60s include toys, comic books, cereal boxes, and yearbooks with atomic names and imagery. One example is a box of Kix cereal from 1947 with a Lone Ranger Atomic Bomb Ring that could be sent to children in exchange for the box top and 15 cents.

Address 755 E Flamingo Road, Las Vegas, NV 89119, +1 (702) 409-7366, www.atomicmuseum.vegas | **Getting there** Bus 202 to EB Flamingo after Palos Verdes or WB Flamingo after University Center | **Hours** Daily 9am–5pm | **Tip** Join a tour of the Nevada National Security Sites, including Sedan Crater and what remains of the Doom Town, on one of the monthly public tours (www.nnss.gov/community/monthly-community-public-tours).

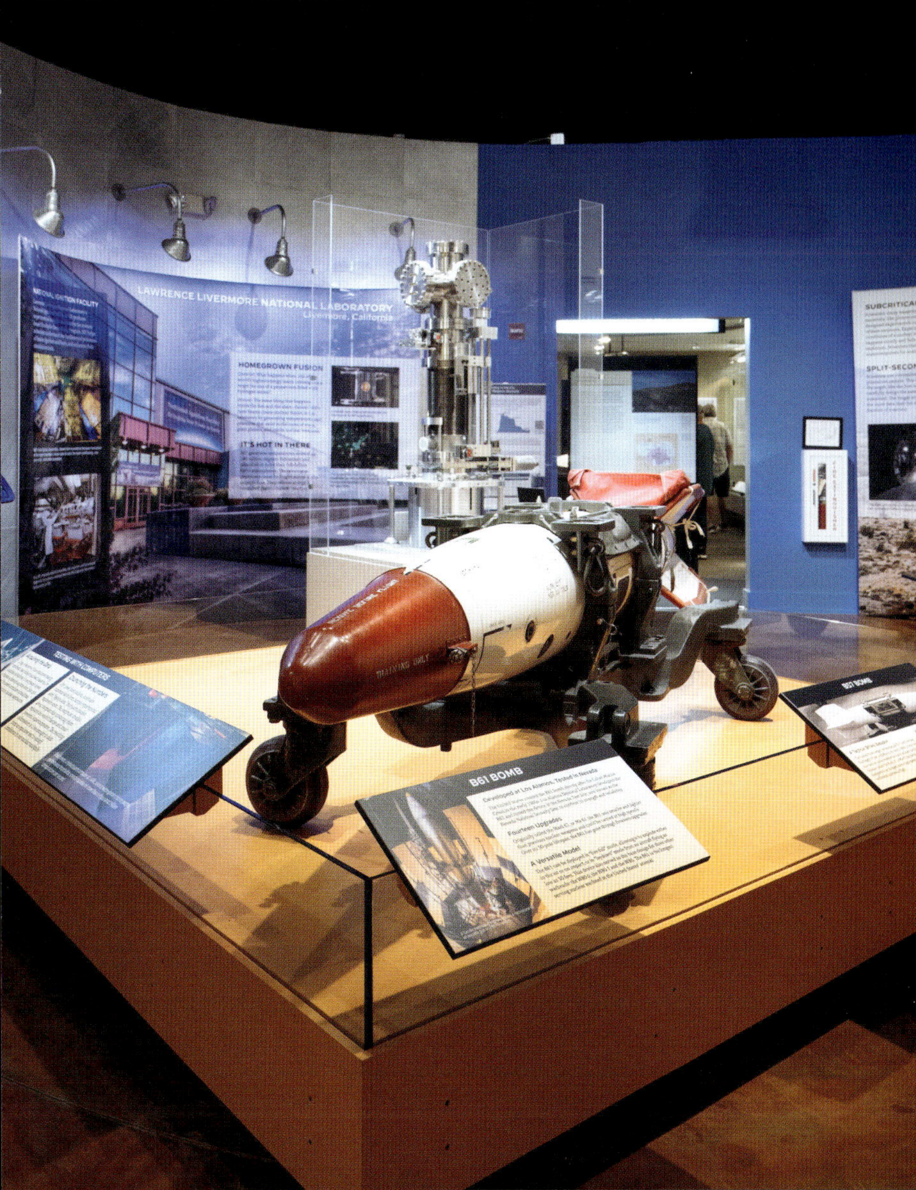

8 Berlin Wall Urinals

A chance to pee on a piece of Cold War history

When the Berlin Wall was officially dismantled in the latter part of 1990, entire sections were preserved. Hundreds of them have been sent around the world, reaching all six inhabited continents, including the distant countries of New Zealand, Japan, South Africa, and Canada.

While many sections are located within museums, universities, or government buildings, some have ended up in much more remarkable places, like the men's bathroom at the Main Street Station Hotel and Casino.

Located near Fremont Street, Main Street Station first opened in 1978 as the Holiday International. Developer Bob Snow, along with Jim Rouse, were approached by the City of Las Vegas in 1985 to undertake a redevelopment of the downtown area. Snow, who also owned Rosie O'Grady's Flying Circus, a skywriting and balloon show, was in Germany during the dismantling of the wall in 1990 and was able to obtain two sections and send them to Las Vegas. He personally oversaw the installation of the wall and when asked why he displayed it in the bathroom, he admitted he thought it would be entertaining.

The bathroom, found on the first floor to the right of the Garden Court Buffet, features four urinals placed on the graffiti-covered wall. A plaque overhead greets the gentlemen entering the bathroom and explains that the wall, created 12 feet high and 18 inches thick, separated Berlin from August 13, 1961 until November 9, 1989. While you technically don't pee on the wall itself, you can metaphorically micturate on an artifact from a dark time in world history. Security can escort those who don't usually use the men's room to get a glimpse and grab a photo.

The rest of Main Street Station features elegant and understated Victorian decor, in stark contrast to the graffiti-laden artifact in its bathroom. This makes the inclusion of the Berlin Wall bathroom even more wonderfully surprising and unexpected.

Address 200 N Main Street, Las Vegas, NV 89101, +1 (702) 387-1896, mainstreet.boydgaming.com | **Getting there** Deuce on the Strip Bus to Stewart & 4th Street or the Downtown Loop Bus to the Mob Museum or Circa | **Hours** Unrestricted | **Tip** Take a self-guided tour of the casino's collection of antiques and curiosities, such as the Louisa May Alcott Pullman car, the chandelier from the Figaro Opera House (Paris, France), and the façade from the Kuwait Royal Bank – maps available at the front desk.

9 The Beverly Theater

Vegas' only independent film house

Las Vegas' entertainment scene is legendary. From music and comedy to acrobatics and burlesque, there are hundreds of events and performances from the colossal arenas to the boutique venues. But when it comes to independent film houses, there's only one. The Beverly Theater, near the Arts District, is a "storytelling headquarters." With a focus on art in all forms, Beverly Theater showcases the film genres "indies, revivals, fests, and moods," literary events with readings, author talks, and Q and As.

The innovative theater opened in 2023, thanks to The Rogers Foundation, the local nonprofit seeking to transform lives through art and education. The theater's namesake, Beverly Rogers, Chairman of the Board for the Rogers Foundation, explained that Las Vegas has never had a true art house and hopes the Beverly Theater gives people an opportunity to experience things they hadn't before in the city. "As a faithful supporter of the arts," she explained, "it's important to me to make sure the community has access to a permanent home for independent film and artistic expression."

At nearly 15,000 square feet, the 140-seat theater (with a 400-person capacity) features advanced technology like a telescopic, retractable seating system; a NanaWall, a moveable glass wall that can open the theater to the courtyard and lobby; and the Constellation, a 17.1 surround audio system by Meyer Sound that can make the room completely neutral, or make it reverberate "like an 18th-century London cathedral," Kip Kelly the theater's chief experience officer told *Las Vegas Weekly*.

But don't call it a "multipurpose" room. Kelly says that makes it sound like a soulless box when, in reality, it's modern and stylish. Exactly the place you want to grab a local craft beer from the concession stand before watching your favorite cult classic or the new film-festival favorite.

Address 515 S 6th Street, Las Vegas, NV 89101, +1 (702) 660-3906, www.thebeverlytheater.com | Getting there Deuce on the Strip Bus to Casino Center at Bonneville Transit Center | Hours Check website for event schedule | Tip See your favorite big screen flicks at West Wind, the last remaining drive-in theater in the valley (4150 W Carey Avenue, North Las Vegas, www.westwinddi.com/locations/las-vegas).

10 Black Sacrament Tattoo

All-female shop with dark and nerdy vibes

Vegas is a hotspot for body art, home to everything from high-traffic walk-in parlors to boutique shops for custom pieces. Black Sacrament Tattoo is a female-owned and run shop by artist Jordan Cole that has become a haven for those seeking an inviting and unique experience. Tattooing first called to Jordan at age 14, when she realized how powerful the art form could be for self-expression. After receiving her third tattoo at 19, she met her mentor, who offered her an apprenticeship, kicking off a career that would ultimately lead to opening her own shop.

But Jordan didn't want to build just another shop in Vegas. She wanted to focus on loyal, local clients who value connection and quality. It's become a favorite for regulars, some of whom even travel from out of state just to be tattooed by the artist they trust. Though Jordan didn't intend for Black Sacrament to be an all-female shop, it evolved naturally. After years of working in male-owned shops, often in environments that were less than welcoming, she realized the importance of creating a healthy, empowering workspace for herself and the talented women she'd met in the industry.

Today, that all-female dynamic is something she and her clients cherish. Many visitors express how safe and comfortable they feel in the studio, something Jordan is deeply proud of. And the studio itself, which Jordan describes as a "spooky cabin," is a reflection of her and her team's personality with cozy and inviting dark, nerdy vibes. Even the name "Black Sacrament" is a nod to one of Jordan's favorite video games: *Elder Scrolls.*

Artistically, Jordan is drawn to realism and illustrative color work, especially florals. Her diverse background in tattooing has made her adaptable, and she now leads a team of versatile artists who can take on nearly any style. There's rarely a request the Black Sacrament crew can't handle.

Address 2585 E Flamingo Road, Las Vegas, NV 89121, +1 (702) 401-7814, www.blacksacramenttattoo.com, blacksacramenttattoo@yahoo.com | **Getting there** Bus 202 to Flamingo after Eastern | **Hours** Daily noon–6pm, by appointment only | **Tip** For the quintessential Vegas tattoo experience, head to the famous Koolsville Tattoo, a favorite for $10 flash tattoos (1232 Las Vegas Boulevard South, www.koolsvilletattoolv.com).

11 Blacksmith Classes

Learn the old ways at the Old Fort

When the Mormons settled in the area, the blacksmith was essential for all aspects of life. The forge was the third building erected, after the hotel and trading post, and focused initially on repairing wagons damaged from the long trip from the Utah Territory. The blacksmith crafted furniture, cooking utensils, weapons, gates, and tools for both themselves and all the other craftsmen needed to establish the community. While we no longer rely on blacksmiths in this way, the art of blacksmithing hasn't been lost. Ramon Fegundo runs classes at the Old Mormon Fort through the Friends of the Fort nonprofit, to teach the "old ways" right at the original settlement.

Fegundo became interested in blacksmithing from the *World of Warcraft* game and martial arts. He saw characters in the game crafting tools and, later, saw the craftsmanship of the katana, a Japanese sword, thinking he would like to be able to do that in real life. He spent over 20 years perfecting his craft while teaching classes at the Fort and in Tonopah, creating metal art, and working as a welder.

With both beginner and advanced classes, students learn to safely light and operate a traditional hand-cranked forge (the blowers date back to the 1910s), the properties of metal, and how to work steel over an anvil. It's truly an art: learning to heat the metal to the perfect red (temperatures are estimated but usually just below 3,000 degrees Fahrenheit), then pounding on an anvil. The process is repeated until the item is finished. One student said the classes are addictive. He came once and was hooked, each time learning more and getting more comfortable and knowledgeable about working the metal. The classes offer a glimpse into an art of the past that is still a useful, and fun, skill to learn today, and each class forges a different item like a wall hook, a bottle opener, a letter opener, or tongs, that can be taken home.

Address 500 E Washington Avenue, Las Vegas, NV 89101, +1 (702) 816-7767, www.friendsofthefort.org, forged.and.fab.metalworks@gmail.com | Getting there Bus 208 to Washington after Main or Bus 113 to Vegas before Tonopah | Hours Check website for class schedule | Tip Learn the skill of jewelry making at the John Fish Jewelry School (953 E Sahara, Suite 5, www.johnfishjewelryschool.com).

12 Blue Angel Sculpture

Iconic piece of downtown history finds a new home

For more than 60 years, the *Blue Angel* sculpture at the Blue Angel Motel on Fremont Street was a landmark for locals. Starting back when young people would cruise up and down Fremont (before the majority was closed to vehicle traffic), they would use the larger-than-life angel as a turnaround point before heading back east to Main Street. Designed by the famed Betty Willis (1923–2015), creator of the "Welcome to Las Vegas" sign, the sculpture first appeared in 1957 at 2110 Fremont Street. The angel greeted guests until the motel's closing in 2011. Even after the motel was demolished in 2015, it remained a symbol of the area until it was removed in 2017 for refurbishment. In 2020, it found its new home just down the street at the five-points corner of Fremont, Charleston, and Eastern, thanks to the Centennial Commission.

Over the years, the 16-foot-tall angel had her skin and hair color altered, a star was added to her wand, and a halo was placed atop her head. Today, the statue has been restored back to the original version that Willis designed, including her gold tassel belt. Another well-known sign also accompanies the angel. The sign for the Blue Onion drive-in restaurant that was located next to the motel has been altered to display "Blue Angel Motel."

While many might consider other signs, sculptures, or architecture more emblematic of Vegas (like the Willis-designed Las Vegas sign), the *Blue Angel* holds a special place in the hearts of Las Vegans. The refurbishment and display of this icon from a bygone era is especially important to a city that has a reputation for destroying and replacing what is no longer commercially successful, often at the cost of history and local sentiment.

Joshua Abbey, former chairman of the City of Las Vegas Arts Commission, told the *Las Vegas Sun*, "She's a powerful symbol of restoration... We need to utilize her powers as a guardian angel to the city."

Address 2450 E Fremont Street, Las Vegas, NV 89104 | Getting there BHX (Boulder Highway Express) Bus to Fremont before Charleston | Hours Unrestricted | Tip Visit another recognizable sculpture marking a business, the Carpeteria Genie, now a mascot for a flooring shop (4221 W Charleston Boulevard).

13 Boulder Dam Hotel

Famed hotel of the Hoover Dam project

The Boulder Dam Hotel, 30 minutes southeast of Las Vegas, was built in 1933 to accommodate guests visiting the construction of the Hoover Dam, then called the Boulder Dam. Paul Stewart "Jim" Webb came up with an idea for an elegant hotel with "unprecedented" private baths and air conditioning, and a luxurious wood-paneled lobby that could accommodate world dignitaries. It was designed in a Colonial Revival style by Henry Smith to feature large columns and windows out front, dramatically different from the architecture of the city then and still today.

The hotel quickly saw success with visitors flocking to the dam and for celebrities who needed to establish residency in Nevada for a quickie divorce (like actor Boris Karloff from his wife Dorothy Stine in 1946). Famous guests during the 1930s included A. P. Giannini, founder of Bank of America; Bette Davis, who stayed at the hotel while on vacation following the filming of *Of Human Bondage*; Will Rogers, who was performing at the Boulder Theatre; Howard Hughes, who recuperated at the hotel after wrecking his plane on Lake Mead; Henry Fonda; Senator Robert Taft; Shirley Temple; and Cardinal Pacelli, who later became Pope Pius XII.

In 1936, the hotel was acquired by Glover "Roxy" Ruckstell and combined with his Grand Canyon-Boulder Dam Tours company, including Grand Canyon Airlines, which offered plane sightseeing tours for only three dollars.

The Dam was closed to visitors during World War II, causing a drastic decrease in guests at the hotel. It struggled to recover financially, moving through multiple owners over the decades. In 1993, "Friends of the Hotel" began renovations and in 2005, Boulder City Museum and Historical Association acquired the hotel to restore it to its former glory. Today, it's a boutique-style hotel with 21 guest rooms that has gained recognition on the National Register of Historic Places.

Address 1305 Arizona Street, Boulder City, NV 89005, +1 (702) 293-3510, www.boulderdamhotel.com | Getting there Bus 221 to Buchanan after Boulder City Parkway | Hours Open 24 hours | Tip Visit the Hoover Dam to get a glimpse into one of the biggest feats of engineering in the world (Hoover Dam Access Road, Boulder City).

14 Broadacres Marketplace

Local flea market celebrating Latino culture

On North Las Vegas Boulevard, about halfway to Nellis Air Force Base, is a sprawling open-air flea market called Broadacres Market. Open on weekends, the market brings together hundreds of local vendors to sell new products, antiques, second-hand goods, and food. You can find refrigerators, new band T-shirts, wheelchairs, vinyl records, knives, and collectible dolls all in one place, what the *Las Vegas Review-Journal* called "a disassembled puzzle spread out in a colorful jumble."

Broadacres began as Broadacres Swap Meet in 1977 when the Bowmans began to sell their produce. The Danz family bought the swap meet in 2007, creating Broadacres Marketplace, which is now more than 40 acres of retail space. Owner Greg Danz said when he came to Las Vegas from California to help his father with their new business, they aimed to create a place where you didn't just go to shop, but where you went to shop and stay a while.

He saw potential for something more, deciding to add stages, a beer bar, and a small amphitheater. After some trial and error, they learned that Latin music with bandas and norteño artists drew the largest crowds. "That's what changed everything," General Manager Yovana Alsonso told the *Review-Journal*, an understatement when more than 1.3 million people visit the market each year.

This truly sets Broadacres apart from other markets or swap meets. The entertainment and family activity factor with new local bands, singers, and performers featured each week as well as kids' attractions like fun carnival rides that spin, twirl, and drop kids to their hearts' content. A trip to the market is more than just about visiting to get things you need – it's an event, an activity that many look forward to each week, and it has evolved into a cultural institution in North Las Vegas. Alonso calls it a home away from home for Latinos, "a piece of Mexico, of Salvador, wherever that community comes from."

Address 2930 Las Vegas Boulevard North, North Las Vegas, NV 89030, +1 (702) 642-3777, www.broadacresm.com | Getting there Bus 113 to Las Vegas at Market Center | Hours Fri 4–11pm, Sat & Sun 6am–5pm | Tip For more local vendors check out Fantastic Indoor Swap Meet to see notable and unusual products (1717 South Decatur, www.fantasticindoorswapmeet.com).

15 Bugsy Siegel Monument

Marker for the mobster who "invented" Las Vegas

Famed New York mobster Benjamin "Bugsy" Siegel is often credited with creating the Las Vegas we know today. His most well-known contribution to Vegas is the Flamingo Las Vegas. As one of the first casinos on the Strip (and today's oldest continuously operating casino in this area), it is often considered an icon that set Las Vegas on its path to the creation of the megaresort.

Although Hollywood developer Billy Wilkerson (1890–1962) started the Flamingo project, Bugsy and his partner, Meyer Lansky (1902–1983), who had been running the El Cortez on Fremont, were brought in after Wilkerson ran low on funding. The stories told from these early days are often debated, with many insisting that Wilkerson be credited with the casino's name, design, and success. However, UNLV history professor Hal Rothman stated in 2000 that Wilkerson's involvement was "more of a footnote. He had an idea but wasn't able to pull it off."

When Bugsy took over the construction of the resort, he set out to create a more modern, cosmopolitan-style hotel, drastically different from the nearby Western-themed resorts El Rancho and Frontier. Bugsy's memorial is now located inside the Flamingo Las Vegas, where the original building stood from 1946 to 1993. Initially consisting of 105 rooms, it had a famous "Bugsy Suite" in the penthouse, which supposedly had four-inch-thick concrete walls and bulletproof windows, and featured multiple secret escape routes. Unfortunately, Siegel didn't get to see the Flamingo come to its full potential because he was killed by an unknown shooter in California in 1947.

While Siegel's name is still seen around Vegas, the Flamingo Las Vegas has since tried to minimize Siegel's involvement, stating he was not a man people should idolize. However, the monument remains, and in 2020 a steakhouse called Bugsy & Meyer's opened on the property and pays homage to the iconic mobsters.

Address 3555 Las Vegas Boulevard South, Las Vegas, NV 89109, +1 (702) 733-3111, www.caesars.com/flamingo-las-vegas | Getting there Deuce on the Strip Bus to Caesars Palace or Harrah's | Hours Daily 7am–8pm | Tip To get a feel for the mob era in Vegas, check out Capo's Italian Restaurant and Speakeasy (5675 W Sahara Avenue, www.caposrestaurant.com).

16_Burlesque Hall of Fame

A dazzling homage to burlesque's rich legacy

Burlesque started in 17th-century France and is best known in its modern form as a variety show that typically features a striptease. American burlesque grew quickly, but by the 1920s, censoring laws were put in place, which caused a swift decline in performances, often making the working conditions harsh and creating a stigma around dancers.

Jennie Lee, a well-known performer in the '50s and '60s, known as "the Bazoom Girl," started The Exotic Dancers' League of North America to help dancers in Los Angeles whose pay was very low and to improve working conditions. Later, the EDL became more of a social organization for retired dancers. Lee began collecting items like G-strings, gowns, pasties, and press pictures to display at the Exotic World Museum at her home in Helendale, California. The museum became a pilgrimage site for both past performers and the new generation of "neo-burlesque" artists who drew inspiration from history to shape their futures. Upon Lee's death in 1991, fellow dancer Dixie Evans took over the museum to keep burlesque and Lee's legacy alive.

Now called the Hall of Fame, the museum is located in the Arts District, after coming to Las Vegas on what should have been a short stop to house its artifacts while the Helendale location was revamped. It has been in Las Vegas since 2006 and continues to hold the annual Miss Exotic World Pageant each June to celebrate past and present performers and fundraise for the Hall of Fame and the preservation of its collection.

The museum is a "living tribute to the raucous, ribald hybrid of music, comedy, theater, and dance, known as burlesque." Visitors can learn about the timeline of burlesque's history and Lee's legacy, and check out vintage posters, photos, costumes, and other memorabilia from a collection of around 4,000 pieces.

Address 1027 S Main Street #110, Las Vegas, NV 89101, +1 (888) 661-6465, www.burlesquehall.com | **Getting there** Deuce on the Strip Bus to Casino Center at Coolidge | **Hours** Fri & Sat 11am–5pm, Sun noon–5pm, Mon 11am–5pm | **Tip** Visit the Las Vegas Showgirl Museum to see wardrobe pieces, sets, and props from iconic shows in Vegas (3217 Gaucho Drive, www.lasvegasshowgirlmuseum.com).

17 Cactus Joe's Nursery

Beloved plant nursery dedicated to desert flora

Cactus Joe's Desert Garden & Nursery is a treasured desert gem just outside of Vegas along Blue Diamond Road. Founded in 1989 by Joe Davidson, the nursery began as a vision to celebrate and preserve the beauty of desert flora. Over time, the seven-acre property transformed into a whimsical, peaceful sanctuary where visitors can connect with nature, art, and the unique ecology of the Mojave Desert. The nursery features an extensive variety of over 300 native and drought-tolerant plant species, including cacti, agaves, succulents, ocotillos, and yuccas. It's also one of Nevada's largest authorized retailers of Joshua trees, a protected species symbolic of the American Southwest.

As a passionate plant enthusiast with a deep respect for sustainable landscaping, Davidson explained to KTNV, "Once established, they could live a year and a half, two years, maybe three years without another drop of water." His nonprofit Desert Love Native Plants works to cultivate more native species not yet available to consumers. "These are beautiful plants that can be grown with tiny amounts of water," he says, something abundantly necessary here in the Mojave with less than five inches of rainfall a year and strict water restrictions in most areas of Las Vegas.

But the nursery has blossomed into more than a place to purchase desert plants. It's a destination, a desert refuge that draws countless locals each year to escape the crowded city and experience the vast open skies of the desert. Besides shopping for the next desert plant for your collection, you can view art installations of life-sized metal dinosaurs or quirky sculptures, pass by a tranquil koi pond, explore a meditation labyrinth, or visit a tiny wedding chapel among the plants. The nursery also hosts events like yoga, meditation sessions, and vendor fairs, all focusing on embracing and protecting desert plant life.

Address 12740 Blue Diamond Road, Las Vegas, NV 89161, +1 (702) 875-1968, www.cactusjoeslv.com, cactusjoeslasvegas@gmail.com | Getting there By car, take Blue Diamond Road (NV-160) West. Turn right to continue onto Blue Diamond Road (NV-159), turn right onto Nursery Street | Hours Mon–Sat 9am–3pm, Sun 10am–3pm | Tip For a more curated and varied plant display, pop over to the popular Bellagio Conservatory for extravagant seasonal displays (3600 Las Vegas Boulevard South, bellagio.mgmresorts.com).

18 Casino Quest

Learn to gamble from the pros, without the risk

Nothing says Las Vegas more than gambling. While slots are an easy and beginner-friendly way to gamble, table games like blackjack and poker are often seen as the pinnacle, with the most action and excitement in the casino. But when each game has dozens of rules and ways to win (adding in table etiquette and casino rules), it can be intimidating and confusing for beginners. That's why Casino Quest is the place to go to learn the ins and outs of gaming.

It was opened by former dealers Alex Kim and David Noll, who also run CEG Dealer School, the largest dealer training school in the world, which trains and places hundreds of dealers in local casinos each month. They also teach gaming rules and techniques on their extremely popular YouTube channel. Both Alex and David have worked in dozens of casinos, as dealers and later supervisors, and have created a team of dealers with real experience in Vegas' major casinos.

The 10,000-square-foot training center is filled with all major gaming tables, some of which were casino-used (like a roulette table from The Mirage). The laid-back atmosphere is the best way to get comfortable with the rules, table etiquette, and techniques for major games like blackjack, poker, baccarat, roulette, and craps at your own pace, from friendly and experienced dealers. It's a great spot to come alone to brush up on techniques or to bring a group of friends for some no-risk fun in a controlled environment. Or, thanks to their established relationships, they can arrange group experiences like no other at local casinos.

Even if you have no intention of pulling up to the blackjack table at Caesars, Casino Quest can be a fun way to "gamble." When you are ready to hit the casinos, you'll be more confident in the rules, have a fun experience (instead of stressing or being confused), and possibly win (though that's not guaranteed).

Address 3100 West Sahara Avenue, Suite 102, Las Vegas, NV 89102, +1 (702) 884-3439, www.casinoquest.biz, sales@casinoquest.biz | Getting there Sahara Express Bus to WB Sahara before Spanish Oaks or EB Sahara before Richfield | Hours Daily 11am–6pm | Tip When you're ready to make some real bets, make your way to the Mandalay Bay Poker Room, often considered the most beginner-friendly in the city (3590 Las Vegas Boulevard South, mandalaybay.mgmresorts.com).

19_Cemetery Pulp

Oddities shop for "the weird and nerdy"

Walking around the Sunset Sands Plaza just east of Harry Reid feels like every other strip mall in Las Vegas. But inside suite 106 is Cemetery Pulp, an oddities shop that is perfectly out of place. Stepping inside is like entering another realm. With comic books, taxidermy, eclectic books, candles, and wet specimens covering every inch of wall and shelf space, all lovers of the weird will find something they need.

Owners Chris Kmit and Erin Emre started out attending trade shows to sell oddities and Emre's taxidermy creations. They soon decided to open a full-time shop for more flexibility and control, but were worried an oddities shop might not succeed on its own. Because many people who like oddities also seem to enjoy comics, they decided to combine the two to draw a wider crowd. But since opening in 2021, they've come to find that their oddities sell far better than their comics and they've been pleasantly surprised with the positive response from visitors and the community.

What sets Cemetery Pulp apart is its taxidermy, all of which was created or restored by Emre, who has been doing taxidermy for over 20 years. The shop features posed squirrels wearing fur coats, mice sitting at a tiny table having tea, and pigs wearing crowns. Many of her specimens are sent from back east and she focuses on not being wasteful, restoring what she can and using all parts of the animal either in the taxidermy, the wet specimens, or in other products like the mystery boxes (by far their best sellers). With categories like bones, insects, and gems, long-time collectors and newbies to oddities alike enjoy choosing a mystery box to see what new items they can own.

Visitors can also find books, pinned butterflies, anatomically correct heart candles, and a full-sized casket to take selfies in, and stop by for Past Life Regression classes, live music nights, and a night market with local artists and vendors.

Address 3950 E Sunset Road, Suite 106, Las Vegas, NV 89120, +1 (725) 206-5412, www.cemeterypulp.com, thefamilyodd@cemeterypulp.com | **Getting there** Bus 212 to Sunset after Sandhill | **Hours** Sat–Mon & Thu 11am–8pm, Tue & Wed 11am–7pm, Fri noon–8pm | **Tip** Visit Nightmare Toys for horror-themed merchandise like clothes, masks, props, and figures (1309 S Commerce Street, www.nightmaretoys.com).

20 Center for Brain Health

A deconstructivist building housing cognitive care

The Cleveland Clinic Lou Ruvo Center for Brain Health, locally referred to as the Brain Health Building, is an unusual and eye-catching structure found on the corner of Grand Central Parkway and Bonneville Avenue in Symphony Park. It is also the home of the Keep Memory Alive foundation, the local nonprofit started by Lou Ruvo's son, Larry Ruvo. The clinic provides world-class Cleveland Clinic care to patients with Alzheimer's, Huntington's, and Parkinson's diseases, multiple sclerosis, multiple system atrophy, and dementia.

Opened in 2010 after three years of construction, its distinctive deconstructionist design sits in stark contrast to the more utilitarian buildings around it. The structure consists of a swirling exterior canopy covering the more traditional orthogonal building. Both the canopy and the interior buildings have a welcoming, light-filled atmosphere. There are over 199 windows, each one unique, and over 18,000 stainless-steel shingles in specific, distinctive measurements.

With a total area of 60,000 square feet, the center provides facilities for all aspects of patient care, research, and education, including an outpatient clinic, neuro-imaging suites, a reference library, community space, multi-purpose event center, a catering kitchen (designed by chef Wolfgang Puck), and office space for Keep Memory Alive.

The center was designed by acclaimed architect Frank Gehry, whose unconventional style can also be seen in the world-renowned Guggenheim Museum in Bilbao, Spain, the Dancing House in Prague, Czech Republic, and the Walt Disney Concert Hall in Los Angeles. "The building symbolizes hope," he said. "Walking into this building took my breath away. I can't remember the last time that happened... somewhere over the rainbow."

Address 888 W Bonneville Avenue, Las Vegas, NV 89106, +1 (702) 232-4547, www.keepmemoryalive.org, delucir@ccf.org | Getting there Deuce on the Strip Bus to Bonneville Transit Center | Hours Unrestricted from the outside, tours by appointment | Tip For other uncommon building design, check out the Veer Towers, residential highrises with a unique tilting design (3726 & 3722 Las Vegas Boulevard South, www.veertowers.org).

21 Charleston Peak Winery

Sip wine at Nevada's largest producer

Pahrump's Charleston Peak Winery is a modern tribute to the region's surprisingly rich winemaking heritage. Local Paiute people have gathered wild grapes for centuries, while the area's viticulture roots go back to the 1880s, when settlers like Aaron and Rosie Winters planted grapevines, and Joseph Yount's Chateau Manse, one of the earliest vineyards, was said "to have been superior to 'California's finest.'"

In the 1990s, Jack Sanders helped usher in the modern era of Nevada wine with the Pahrump Valley Winery, which in 2005 produced the state's first commercial red wine, made from locally grown Zinfandel grapes. This milestone established Pahrump as a viable region for winemaking despite the desert landscape. In fact, the arid climate and intense sun produce bold, flavorful grapes that result in a singularly rich, vibrant wine unlike from any other region.

Pahrump Valley Winery, now Charleston Peak Winery, has been called an "iconic staple" in Pahrump. The sprawling 10-acre estate was built in 1989 and has produced wine since 1992. The winery "holds a special place in the hearts of many longtime residents," according to *Pahrump Valley Community News*. General Manager Jenn Sela Bowen is breathing new life into the property while still "preserving the legacy that made the winery a beloved destination." Owner and winemaker, Steve Bowen, brings experience from Napa Valley, introducing new wines like a Malbec with grapes sourced in Dyer and red blends from Amargosa, which are distinctive thanks to the desert climate and unique soil found in Pahrump and around Nevada. But old favorites like the Symphony and Desert Blush varieties are still available to honor the property's legacy. Beyond the production, the winery is focused on creating an elevated wine-education experience. "It's about creating a memorable and educational experience for everyone who walks through our doors."

Address 3810 Winery Road, Pahrump, NV 89048, +1 (775) 751-7800, www.charlestonpeakwinery.com, info@charlestonpeakwinery.com | Getting there By car, take NV-160 West to Winery Road | Hours Thu–Mon noon–5pm | Tip On the way back to Vegas, stop by to Spring Mountain Ranch State Park to see some of the oldest buildings in Nevada and a luxury retreat for German actress Vera Krupp and later billionaire Howard Hughes (6375 NV-159, Blue Diamond, www.parks.nv.gov/parks/spring-mountain-ranch).

22 Cliff's Barber Corral

Barber with an Old West flair

A strip mall on East Tropicana feels like an odd place for an Old West barber shop. But among the nondescript storefronts sprouts a lush cactus garden in front of Cliff's Barber Corral. Owner Cliff Wolosin has been barbering since 1964. His grandfather, a barber by trade, suggested that Cliff learn the skill, so he used his GI Bill benefits to go to Long Beach Barber College and hasn't looked back since.

Cliff worked in Culver City, California, near many big movie studios, cutting the hair of movie stars and musicians like Freddie Mercury before coming out to Vegas in 1996. His shop draws in customers with the outlandish theme. It holds a varied collection of antiques and trinkets from the Old West, including a vintage sewing table, taxidermy, Native American artifacts, and old-school barbers' chairs. The space is packed with items from floor to ceiling, both in the shop itself and in the front gallery, making you feel like you've gone back in time before heading in for a classic haircut. Most items have been gifted or donated to Cliff by friends or dedicated customers, with him saying every item has a story.

But beyond the decor, Cliff and his team are talented barbers who keep people coming back. "Barbering is a very individual performance," Cliff explains. "Everybody goes to the same school, but it's what we do with what we learn that casts us to be so different. And I had this desire to be, not good, but the best barber ever. And I wanted to show that I could do this." One of Cliff's signature techniques includes using giant scissors. He liked them because they were different and special, but also quicker and more accurate. The heavy scissors tired his hands, so he started twirling his scissors, stretching his fingers, and creating a dramatic, fun display for the customers. "I just like my job," Cliff continues. "And I like people to like my haircut."

Address 3330 E Tropicana Avenue, #A, Las Vegas, NV 89121, +1 (702) 456-7300, www.cliffsbarbercorral.com | Getting there Bus 111 to Pecos after Tropicana | Hours Daily 9am–7pm | Tip For another barber experience, try out the Speakeasy Barbershop at El Cortez to get a haircut in a shop with old Vegas vibes and a deep history (600 East Fremont Street, www.elcortezhotelcasino.com).

23 Coffinwood

Coffin-shaped oasis in the heart of the desert

In Pahrump, the unincorporated town just 40 minutes from Las Vegas, you can find Coffinwood, a peculiar and eccentric attraction. Serving as both the home and business of Bryan and Dusty Schoening, it is renowned for its coffin-shaped architecture, including a gazebo, garden planters, and even a pet cemetery, all contributing to its distinctive appearance.

Coffinwood began after a personal tragedy. In 1997, Bryan's parents and family dog were killed by an impaired driver. This experience led Bryan to become disillusioned with the funeral industry. "It was horrific enough losing his parents in such a tragic way, and then to go through all of that and just feel guilted into [buying something expensive] was horrible," Dusty told the *Las Vegas Review-Journal*. While this was the inspiration, the real catalyst for Coffin It Up (his primary coffin-making business) came in 2000 when his daughter and her friend asked Bryan, a trained cabinet-maker, to make them a coffin for a Halloween prank. "I thought I could build them a coffin in one day," Bryan said. "Four days later, I am still figuring out how to do the angles. I became addicted to that challenge." Coffins, which have six or eight sides, more closely resemble a human, compared to the more standard box-like caskets. The United States is one of the few countries that uses caskets, making coffins a novelty to many, or something associated with Halloween or a haunted house.

Visitors to Coffinwood can explore various attractions, including a collection of hearses; a lapidary studio; the Church of the Coffin, where Bryan, an ordained minister, performs weddings; the Coffinwood Cemetery and Wildlife Habitat; and their mascot, Tank, a rescued African tortoise. While the property is a private residence, the Schoenings welcome visitors to experience their artistic, life-affirming creations during their scheduled tours.

Address 2875 Sunset Street, Pahrump, NV 89060, +1 (775) 209-4998, www.coffinwoodpahrump.com, coffinitup@yahoo.com | Getting there By car, take NV-160 West, turn left onto E Mesquite Avenue, then right onto N Barney Street, and finally right onto Sunset Street | Hours Tours Sun 8am, 10am & 2pm | Tip Grab a slice of pizza and view an impressive collection of Evel Knievel memorabilia and artifacts at one of the top pizza shops in the city, Evel Pie (508 Fremont Street, www.evelpie.com).

24 Cold War National Memorial

Hidden heroes honored at Mount Charleston

Just outside the Spring Mountains Visitor Gateway is the country's first national memorial dedicated exclusively to the Cold War's covert personnel: military, intelligence, and civilians whose clandestine efforts were pivotal in maintaining national security during this era.

The memorial's origins go back to November 17, 1955, when USAF Flight 9068 crashed into Mount Charleston's rugged terrain. The C-54 aircraft was en route from Burbank, California, to an area now known as Area 51, carrying 14 people: four Air Force crew members, five CIA personnel, and five engineers and technicians from Lockheed and Hycon who were engaged in the development of the secret U-2 reconnaissance aircraft. For decades, the crash site remained unmarked, and the identities of those aboard were classified.

In 1998, local Boy Scout leader Steve Ririe discovered remnants of the wreckage during a hike. Through declassified documents and archival research, Ririe identified the 14 men and informed their families, many of whom were unaware of what their loved ones had done or how they had died. Ririe then proposed the creation of a memorial to honor the individuals and all Cold War personnel who served in secrecy.

With support from Senator Harry Reid and the US Forest Service, the Silent Heroes of the Cold War Memorial was dedicated on May 29, 2015. The memorial features a twisted propeller from the crashed aircraft, surrounded by 14 stones representing each individual lost. A vault beneath the memorial contains personal mementos from the victims' families, symbolizing the closure they never received. "The patriots this memorial will honor are not forgotten heroes. They're heroes who had their history erased," Ririe told the *Las Vegas Review-Journal*. "The people who worked in secret did so," he said, "so they wouldn't be recognized. This will be a first step to give them back their place in history."

Address 2525 Kyle Canyon Road, Mount Charleston, NV 89124, +1 (702) 872-5486, www.gomtcharleston.com | **Getting there** By car, take I-11/US-95 N to exit 96 toward Kyle Canyon Road. Continue to the Visitor Gateway | **Hours** Daily 9am–4pm | **Tip** Also visit the Veterans Memorial Wall inscribed with the names of more than 1,900 veterans who were Henderson residents at the time of their service or Henderson residents killed in action (240 S Water Street, Henderson, www.cityofhenderson.com).

25 Community Healing Garden

A serene spot for hope and reflection

What was once a vacant lot on the corner of Casino Center and Charleston is now an oasis dedicated to healing, remembrance, and reflection. Jay Pleggenkuhle and Daniel Perez of Stonerose Landscapes sketched out an idea for a memorial garden on a napkin just hours after 58 people were killed and more than 500 others injured by a gunman at the Route 91 Harvest Festival near the Mandalay Bay Casino on October 1, 2017. The memorial opened just five days later.

The project was completed by hundreds of volunteers – UNLV students, local residents, and businesses – using only donated supplies, including plants, wood, and even an irrigation system. From people planting trees and laying bricks to donating pizza and coffee for volunteers, the citizens of Las Vegas came together in the aftermath of the worst tragedy the city has ever seen. "This is the best of the city of Las Vegas," City Attorney Brad Jerbic told KCLV. "This is about as organic and genuine as it comes."

The garden includes a Wall of Remembrance, a grove of trees, shrubs, flowers, walkways of pavers, and benches. The original Remembrance Wall was made of wood pallets covered in handwritten names and dedications. It has since been replaced with a permanent wall made of steel to ensure it will withstand the hot desert sun.

The oak tree in the middle of the garden, donated by magician duo Siegfried and Roy, is known as the Tree of Life. The tree is in a heart-shaped planter adorned with tiles made by the victims' families, survivors, and community members. A winding path leads from the entrance to this central tree, with exactly 58 trees lining the path, each dedicated to a victim who passed. Open all year, the beautiful garden is a place of refuge, a place to remember, a place to reflect, and a lasting symbol of a community coming together after heartbreak.

Address 1015 S Casino Center Boulevard, Las Vegas, NV 89101, +1 (702) 997-3350, www.lasvegasnevada.gov/residents/parks-facilities/community-healing-garden | Getting there Deuce on the Strip Bus to Casino Center at Coolidge | Hours Daily 7am–11pm | Tip Visit Siegfried and Roy Park for walking paths and playgrounds not far from the Strip (5525 S Maryland Parkway).

26 Corn Creek Springs

Landmark railroad-tie home on the wildlife refuge

Between 1905 and 1918, the Las Vegas and Tonopah Railroad passed just two miles from Corn Creek, a small community north of Las Vegas in what is now the Desert National Wildlife Refuge (DNWR). This area had been home to the Nuwuvi (Southern Paiute) people for thousands of years and was later a ranch for homesteaders beginning in the late 19th century, due to its being one of the few places in the desert to find water. Corn Creek became a typical stopping point for the steam-powered locomotives as they moved miners out to Beatty, Bullfrog, Rhyolite, and Goldfield to gather water for fuel before heading into the dry and unforgiving desert.

When the mining industry dwindled, the railroad was abandoned. Because wood is scarce in the desert, the discarded ties became building materials for homes, fence posts, and tools.

Built in 1920 by the Richardson family, this railroad tie cabin served as a home for Dick Richardson (the teenage son who wanted a separate space from his parents). Unlike a traditional notched log cabin, which uses grooves cut into the wood to hold it together, the railroad ties are held together with railroad spikes. Dick lived in the cabin until 1939 when the US Fish and Wildlife Service bought the land to be used for the wildlife refuge. The DNWR was established to protect Southern Nevada's wildlife, most notably the desert bighorn sheep, the state mammal. At 1.6 million acres, it is the largest wildlife refuge in the contiguous United States.

The cabin is still on the refuge along the easy Coyote Loop trail just outside the visitor center. It was restored in 2007 by the United States Fish and Wildlife Service (USFWS) to clean up and preserve the structure, which is sometimes used for education activities. Today it is a great reminder of the early industrialism of Southern Nevada and the resourcefulness of people living in the harsh and often uninhabitable landscape.

Address 16001 Corn Creek Road, Las Vegas, NV 89124, +1 (702) 879-6110, www.fws.gov/refuge/desert, desertcomplex@fws.gov | **Getting there** By car, take 95 North towards Tonopah then turn right onto Corn Creek Road | **Hours** Daily dawn–dusk | **Tip** Continue on 95 N to Rhyolite Ghost Town, the most photographed ghost town in the West (Rhyolite Road, Beatty, www.nps.gov/deva/learn/historyculture/rhyolite-ghost-town.htm).

27 CSN Planetarium

View stars, shows, and NASA artifacts

The Dale Etheridge Planetarium, on the North Las Vegas campus of the College of Southern Nevada (CSN), is the only public planetarium in Southern Nevada (and one of only two in the entire state). Serving the university's astronomy classes (and available for use by any class on campus), it is open to the public, offering the community educational lessons on astronomy, history, biology, and chemistry, as well as entertainment programs.

The planetarium was established in 1977, in major part due to Dr. Dale Etheridge, in whose honor the theater was renamed following his passing in 2019. Dr. Etheridge was a founding member of the Pacific Planetarium Society and served as the planetarium director and professor of astronomy at CSN from 1976 to 2014. The planetarium was "not just where he worked but a tool for showing the universe to everyone."

The 66-seat theater features a 30-foot dome with an Evans & Sutherland Digistar 5 high definition hemispheric video-projection system that creates an immersive experience for the 40-plus shows in the catalog. Open for rotating scheduled shows on weekends, they also hold meditation Mondays for CSN students, school field trips, the free Story Time Under the Stars, special community STEM events, guest lectures, and private events. One huge draw to the planetarium was its show based on Pink Floyd's *Dark Side of the Moon*. It was its most popular show to date, and Planetarium Manager Dr. Andrew Kerr called it the best audio-visual experience he's seen.

Visitors can also view the Astronaut Hall of Fame and NASA artifacts including a tire from the Space Shuttle Discovery, which Planetarium Coordinator Lisa Goodman says has been a big hit, especially with students, who love to be able to touch an object that has been in space.

Address 3200 E Cheyenne Avenue, Building S, North Las Vegas, NV 89030, +1 (702) 651-4759, csnplanetarium.square.site, planetarium@csn.edu | Getting there Bus 113 to 3rd Las Vegas after Pecos or Las Vegas after Cheyenne | Hours See website for current program schedule | Tip Visit Nevada's first astronomy route connecting two Dark Sky Parks (Death Valley and Great Basin) called Park to Park in the Dark, nicknamed the Starry-est Route in America (US-95 and US-6 between Death Valley and Great Basin National Parks, www.parktoparkinthedark.org).

28 Desert Princess Riverboat

Mississippi riverboat on Lake Mead

Lake Mead, the man-made lake created by the Hoover Dam, is located within Lake Mead National Recreation Area, the nation's most diverse NRA. The lake is a favorite of locals looking to beat the desert heat by heading out on the water. While many choose to kayak, swim, or bring out their own boats, the *Desert Princess* riverboat is a fun and relaxing way to experience the lake while learning about the area, the history of the dam, and the growth of Southern Nevada.

As the largest vessel on Lake Mead, it's an authentic Mississippi-style paddle wheeler built specifically to give sightseeing tours of the lake and the backside of the Hoover Dam. Operated by Lake Mead Cruises, this three-decker ship can fit 270 passengers. It's equipped with a full bar and surprisingly large food menu, so you can snack while watching the scenery go by, get a view of the Hoover Dam and the Mike O'Callaghan-Pat Tillman Bridge, and hear about the geological and historical significance of Lake Mead and the Hoover Dam through the on-board commentary.

While having a Mississippi riverboat on Lake Mead seems odd, these classic steamboats have been found along rivers in the Southwest since the mid 1800s. Primarily used for transporting people and goods from settlements near the Pacific Ocean, they operated mostly between the Colorado River Delta, the Gulf of California in Mexico, and up to the Virgin River of Southern Nevada. One of the most well-known steamships along the Colorado River was the *Explorer*, on which noted historian Lt. Joseph Christmas Ives explored from the Grand Canyon up to the Virgin River in 1855. Ives traveled through a portion of the Colorado River that later became Lake Mead after the construction of the Hoover Dam. The Iconic rear paddles of the boat give the experience an old-world feel, something completely different from the modern and ever-changing experience in most of Las Vegas.

Address 490 Horsepower Cove, Boulder City, NV 89005, +1 (702) 293-6180, www.lakemeadcruises.com, emaillakemead@aramark.com | Getting there By car, take I-11 S toward Boulder. Take exit 15B for US-93. Turn left onto Lakeshore Road and then right onto Hemenway Road toward Lake Mead Marina | Hours Check website for cruise schedule | Tip For another lake experience, travel over to Lake Las Vegas for paddle boarding, kayaking, boat rentals, and more (Costa Di Lago, Henderson).

29 The Dinosaur House

Home overtaken by prehistoric paraphernalia

If you're in Henderson and suddenly find yourself face-to-face with a herd of dinosaurs in someone's front yard, you've stumbled upon the legendary Dinosaur House, or Shan-Gri-La Prehistoric Park. This wonderfully weird attraction is the creation of Steve Springer. Known around town as "Dinoman," he's a retired middle school English teacher of 30 years with a heart for education, creativity, and spreading joy.

Steve's journey to dino-fame began in 2005 when a catalog image of a dinosaur caught his eye. At the time, his yard was an eclectic mix of unicorns, aliens, and yeti sculptures, but that one spark set off what would become a full-blown prehistoric paradise. By 2006, his vision was born with the simple mission: "Teach about the past to preserve the present and protect the future," but also "provide smiles and joy to all visitors."

The unicorns are long gone, replaced by over 60 dinosaurs and mythical creatures, including sea serpents, dragons, giant ants, and four enormous tortoises anchoring each corner of the driveway. The park's centerpiece is "Tex," a 27-foot-long Tyrannosaurus rex who often clutches something amusing (or alarming) in his mouth. Tex is joined by a wild crew of triceratops, velociraptors, brontosauruses, stegosauruses, and even baby dinos hatching from eggs. Springer constantly adds new elements, and decorates for holidays, transforming the park for events like Halloween (which can draw over 2,500 trick-or-treaters) and Valentine's Day.

The Dinosaur House welcomes more than 40,000 visitors a year, including local kids, school field trips, and curious tourists, who come to view and learn about dinosaurs and prehistoric figures, or just see the impressive collection. When you're around town, look out for Springer's dinosaur-themed car, the Dinomobile, with "DINOMAN" on the license plate and yell, "Hey, Dinoman!" You might just get a free dinosaur.

Address 733 Greenway Road, Henderson, NV 89002, +1 (702) 565-4645, www.shangrilaprehistoricpark.org | Getting there Bus 221 to Horizon before Jade or Horizon after Greenway | Hours Fall/Winter/Spring Fri–Sun noon–4pm, Summer Fri–Sun 9am–1pm | Tip Check out the exterior (and sometimes open-house) of the former home of Lonnie Hammargren, the former Lieutenant Governor of Nevada and eccentric collector, which has been called "the craziest house in the world" (4318 Ridgecrest Drive, Las Vegas).

30 Discovery Children's Museum

A three-story journey of fun, learning, and wonder

Las Vegas is home to more than 200,000 children, and visitors remain shocked children exist in a city built on adult entertainment. Though museums, parks, and kid-centered businesses are dotted around the valley, few are solely dedicated to children and their education. Discovery Children's Museum, what *Travel Nevada* described as a "creative buffet" for kids, is a 58,000-square-foot, three-story building, packed with exhibits that promote play and exploration for ages 0–13.

Founded by film and TV producer Robin Greenspun (daughter of *Las Vegas Sun* founder Hank Greenspun) and lawyer Mark Tratos in 1984, its aim was to create a much-needed educational institution in the city. The museum opened in 1990, expanding to its current location in Symphony Park in 2013 thanks to a partnership with the Donald W. Reynolds Foundation.

The museum includes nine interactive exhibits accessible via a central play structure with stairs, slides, and bridges. Under fives can head to Toddler Town while drama lovers can visit Fantasy Festival, with costumes and interactive sets. Artists can head to Young at Art to get messy and hone their creativity. Test out careers at a hospital, grocery store, airport, auto shop, bank, and even the Raiders Stadium at Eco City, or learn about energy generation, use, and storage at Energy/Energía. Get ideas for new patents at Patents Pending, a lab-like environment where you can experiment, tinker, and solve design and engineering challenges. The Discovery Lab, an innovative maker space lets kids build and take risks, but universal favorite, Water World, is an interactive exhibit that teaches the power and preciousness of water. The exciting and energetic environment is perfect for kids looking to explore and make messes, while letting someone else clean it up. As the museum says, "from their first day of school to their first a-ha moments."

Address 360 Promenade Place, Las Vegas, NV 89106, +1 (702) 382-3445, www.discoverykidslv.org, info@discoverykidslv.org | Getting there Centennial Express Bus to Bonneville before Promenade | Hours Tue–Sat 10am–5pm, Sun noon–5pm | Tip Check out the Museum of Illusions for mind-bending exhibits both kids and adults will love (3716 Las Vegas Boulevard South, #1.02, www.moilasvegas.com).

31 Dulceria La Colmena

Latin American treats, piñatas, and goods

Las Vegas has a mix of residents from all over the world. Along with these residents come businesses that cater to the diverse communities. One of those places is Dulceria La Colmena, found on Craig Road in North Las Vegas. Started by the Ortega family in 2018, it sought to bring the extraordinary flavors of Latin America to Las Vegas with its stock of candies, chocolates, piñatas, party supplies, condiments, and snacks.

But beyond physically supplying the area with goods, the shop keeps Hispanic culture alive. "Hispanics come into the store to find their childhood favorites, and others in Las Vegas get to experience the culture here," Albert Ortega, a spokesperson for Dulceria la Colmena, told *Best of Las Vegas*. He goes on to tell a story about how they helped a long-term customer find a candy "he had not been able to find since he moved to America, more than 25 years ago... We were able to get it for him, and he was overwhelmed with gratitude and joy," Ortega said.

The name "Dulceria La Colmena" translates to "Honeycomb Candy Shop," reflecting both the sweet treats they sell and the sense of community they've fostered.

Their handmade piñatas, one of the shop's top sellers, are displayed outside as well as all over the ceiling inside. Along with the balloons, party supplies, and giant packs of candies, it's like stepping inside a party with hundreds of treats to choose from. Ortega's favorite is the Vero Mango lollipop. It's a classic Mexican candy shaped like a mango and covered with chili. It's a popular candy that evokes a sense of nostalgia for many adults who remember it from their childhood. He, in particular, has fond memories of enjoying the sweet and spicy lollipops as a kid. Whether looking to find a nostalgic favorite from childhood, to try a new treat, or to get supplies for your next party, Dulceria La Colmena is well worth the trip to North Las Vegas.

Address 3853 E Craig Road, Suite 9, North Las Vegas, NV 89030, +1 (702) 664-2388, www.dulceriacolmena.com, inbox@dulceriacolmena.com | Getting there Bus 219 to EB Craig after Pecos or WB Craig before Mitchell | Hours Mon–Sat 9am–7pm | Tip For more Mexican treats, visit the wildly popular Tacos El Gordo (3041 Las Vegas Boulevard South, www.tacoselgordobc.com).

32 El Cortez Hotel and Casino

The longest-running casino in Las Vegas

In the 1930s and '40s, the downtown area near Fremont began to flourish, opening bars and casinos to cater to visitors wanting to take part in the recently legalized gambling in Nevada. When the El Cortez first opened in 1941, only the Hotel Nevada (later the Sal Sagev, now the Golden Gate), the Las Vegas Club, The Northern Club, and a few saloons could be found around Fremont Street. Mobsters Bugsy Siegel, Moe Sedway, Gus Greenham, and Meyer Lansky bought El Cortez in 1945 to use it to train employees who would go on to open the Flamingo in 1946.

Unlike most businesses in Las Vegas, El Cortez has remained a constant. It is still family run (something exceptional in Las Vegas) and has never changed the name, general design, or exterior façade, keeping the same signage and Spanish ranch-themed architecture. Due to this, it was placed on the Register of Historic Places in 2013, making it the first and only still-operating casino on the list.

El Cortez has expanded in recent years, most notably the 1980 expansion of the 15-story hotel tower behind the property. Owner Jackie Gaughan and his wife Bertie lived in the private penthouse for more than 30 years until Jackie's death in 2014. One of the most notable refurbishments are the "Original 47" rooms. Opened in 2022, the rooms are themed to the style of what they would have been in 1941 when Siegel, Lansky et al owned the property. Located just a single staircase above the casino floor (another unheard of thing in today's Las Vegas), these rooms may have been where Siegel and Lansky stayed while overseeing the business. They are a throwback to a different era of Las Vegas, with bright teal walls, mid-century modern furniture, and art from the '40s and '50s. Visitors looking to get a taste of Vegas from this bygone era will love experiencing these glamorous rooms.

Address 600 E Fremont Street, Las Vegas, NV 89101, +1 (702) 385-5200, www.elcortezhotelcasino.com | **Getting there** Deuce on the Strip Bus to 4th at Fremont Street Experience or Downtown Loop Bus to Fremont East Entertainment District | **Hours** Open 24 hours | **Tip** Visit another of the oldest properties on Fremont, the Golden Gate, and see the plaque commemorating Las Vegas' first telephone (1 Fremont Street, www.goldengatecasino.com).

33 Featherblade Craft Butchery

The city's only sustainable butcher shop

Featherblade Craft Butchery on the corner of West Charleston and Durango has quickly carved out a name for itself in the Las Vegas culinary scene. Founded by London-born butcher Martin Kirrane, Featherblade brings a distinctly British approach to meat, driven by full-animal butchery and an unwavering commitment to ethical sourcing.

In London, Kirrane was just one of many traditional butchers. "Small fish in a big pond," he said of his previous ventures. But in Vegas, where independent butcher shops are rare, his craft immediately stood out. Since opening in 2021, Featherblade has drawn attention from local chefs and curious foodies alike. Featherblade partners with local sustainable producers like Las Vegas Livestock, Strauss Brands, and Santa Carota, ensuring their offerings meet high standards for animal welfare.

Behind the counter, Kirrane and his team – all with backgrounds in professional kitchens – prepare specialty cuts using traditional English techniques and commit to whole animal butchery, meaning they break down the entire animal, rather than working with pre-cut sections, to use as much of the animal as possible to minimize waste. Customers can find British classics like bangers, Cumberland sausages, and back bacon, alongside familiar selections like St. Louis-style ribs, local pork tenderloin, and Creekstone Farms prime beef.

Adding a delicious touch to the experience, the shop's hot box is filled with delicious-smelling sausage rolls and Cornish pasties. Plus, shop their freezer section for succulent English meat pies to take home or various organ meats for your more adventurous recipes. This mix of quality, tradition, and community spirit has quickly made Featherblade a local favorite. "We know about a third of our customers by name," Kirrane says, a testament to the personal touch that sets Featherblade apart, especially in as big a city as Vegas.

Address 8550 W Charleston Boulevard, Suite 104, Las Vegas, NV 89117, +1 (702) 625-2733, www.featherbladeusa.com, hello@featherbladeusa.com | Getting there Bus 206 to Charleston after Durango | Hours Mon–Fri 10am–6pm, Sat 10am–5:30pm, Sun 10am–3:30pm | Tip Visit John Mull's Road Kill Grill for another butcher and some of the best BBQ in the city (3730 Thom Boulevard, www.johnmullsmeatcompany.com).

34 Fergusons Downtown

Shop local at a bygone motel #rootedin community

With the rise of megaresorts, Las Vegas' local businesses have been all but wiped out. But in recent years, there has been a concerted effort to revitalize Las Vegas, specifically the downtown area surrounding the Fremont Street Experience that was once a thriving community hub. Fergusons Downtown, once the historic Fergusons Motel, is now home to a dozen local small businesses. The revitalized open-air motel just a few blocks away from Fremont's attractions is a community space that features shops, a large grass area for events, and room for stage performances. "The more you spend locally, that money goes back into your local economy," Fergusons Downtown founder Jen Taler told 9 News Now.

The building itself has kept its mid-century modern architecture but has been updated to feel new and elegant. The motel's centerpiece is *The Big Rig Jig* by Mike Ross, an art installation featuring interconnected tanker trucks that debuted at Burning Man in 2007.

Visitors can see some of the motel's shops like Mike's Recovery, All For Our Country, LV Plant Collective, and D. Rene & Co., which all sell locally made and sourced goods. Fergusons Downtown is also home to Tofu Tees. Founded in 2016 by then-eight-year-old activist and artist Kumei Norwood, the shop sells stickers, pins, apparel, and homeware featuring phrases and slogans supporting various social issues. Tofu Tees also features a regular "Black Owned" market that highlights Black makers and artists in the community year round.

One big draw of the motel is Mothership Coffee, a locally owned shop with locations around the valley that won the Small Business Administration's 2023 Small Business of the Year award. Fergusons Downtown also holds events like live music, competitions, community Hey Maker markets, and classes (try one of F the Bar's cocktail classes).

Address 1028 Fremont Street, Las Vegas, NV 89101, www.fergusonsdowntown.com | Getting there Deuce on the Strip Bus to Fremont Street Experience or the Downtown Loop Bus to Fremont East Entertainment District | Hours Mon–Wed 8am–5pm, Thu–Sun 8am–10pm | Tip For more shopping and dining in a quirky location, head to The Container Park (707 East Fremont Street) for shops housed in repurposed shipping containers.

35 First Statue of Liberty

The city's original and lesser-known Lady Liberty

New York City's Statue of Liberty has hundreds of replicas worldwide. From Paris to Tokyo, and even a few in Buffalo, New York, but one of the more famous replicas is in front of the New York-New York Hotel & Casino in Las Vegas. This half-sized replica (standing at 150 feet tall) is the largest replica and an iconic waypoint along the Strip. The statue, created by sculptor Robert Davidson, is more "fresh-faced, sultry, and even sexier," than the original according to his attorneys. These terms were used in court when Davidson sued the US Postal Service after his statue was mistakenly placed on three billion postage stamps in circulation for three months in 2011 before the blunder was discovered.

But what many don't know is that Vegas is home to another Statue of Liberty. Found at the aptly named Liberty Square on West Sahara Avenue, this statue has been residing over the businesses here since 1981, 16 years before the opening of New York-New York Hotel & Casino. The now seedy strip mall, home to stores selling exotic shoes and "sweet seduction bikinis," seems an unlikely location for a Liberty replica. The graffitied sign out front that once promoted tax services completes the look of a neighborhood that has seen better days. Like when the base of the statue was used as a pizza drive-thru for Liberty Pizza, or so it's told by Las Vegas expert James Reza.

But Lady Liberty herself remains in great shape, despite her age, and stands as a beacon over the square that sells items perhaps very fitting of Las Vegas' stereotypical appeal for many. While the larger Liberty at New York-New York remains the more widely-known and sought-after of the two that call Las Vegas home, the West Sahara replica deserves a visit, if only to see an iconic American symbol in an implausible location. As *Roadside America* said, "It's hard to not smile at first sight of its towering replica of the Statue of Liberty."

Address 4201 W Sahara Avenue, Las Vegas, NV 89102 | Getting there SX-A Sahara Express to Sahara after Las Verdes | Hours Unrestricted from the outside | Tip Visit the New York-New York Hotel & Casino to experience the New York-themed Cirque du Soleil show *Mad Apple* (3790 Las Vegas Boulevard South, newyorknewyork.mgmresorts.com).

36 Four-Faced Brahma Shrine

The only Brahma shrine in the Western world

Phra Phrom, known outside of Thailand as the Four-Faced Brahma, is the Thai representation of the Hindu creator god Brahma. Each head represents the Four Divine States of Mind: Loving Kindness, Compassion, Sympathy, and Equanimity, with each side offering different blessings.

Brahma statues can be found in China, Singapore, Indonesia, Malaysia, Taiwan, and Thailand. But the most well-known shrine is the Erawan Shrine in Bangkok, which was built in 1956 outside of the government-owned Erawan Hotel to eliminate the bad karma thought to have been created by the laying of the foundation on the wrong date. While shrines to Brahma are common across Asia, the only one in the Western world can be found outside of Caesars Palace in Vegas. Modeled after the Erawan Shrine, it was gifted to the resort in 1984 by Thai newspaper mogul Kamphol Vacharaphol, his wife, and leading Hong Kong gambling tycoon Mr. Yip Hon.

The statue's casting ceremonies were held in Bangkok on November 25, 1983, and many important religious authorities and international dignitaries participated. Cast in bronze, the statue is gold-plated, and its housing is precast concrete covered in beveled glass pieces. The entire statue was shipped to Las Vegas in pieces and assembled here. Caesars held dedication ceremonies on February 5, 1984, that were overseen by Buddhist monks and included a troupe of 21 Thai dancers and musicians.

Worshipers of the god usually offer incense, candles, jasmine flowers, or jasmine garlands in their worship, placing the offerings before each of the four heads. It is also customary to place small elephants at the shrine, which visitors can see around the bottom. Caesars has incense available at the shrine and places to kneel in front of each of the four sides of the shrine. Donations at the shrine are given to charities in Thailand.

Address 3570 Las Vegas Boulevard South, Las Vegas, NV 89109 | Getting there Deuce on the Strip Bus to Caesars Palace Hotel & Casino | Hours Unrestricted | Tip For those interested in the Hindu religion, the Hindu and Jain Temple of Las Vegas is a great place to start (1701 Sageberry Drive, www.hindutemplelv.org).

37_Gamblers General Store

Shop at the world's largest gambling supply shop

On the corner of Main Street and Gass is a mural-covered building that might be easy to pass by despite its exterior of Las Vegas and gambling iconography. But Gamblers General Store is the largest supplier of gambling supplies in the world. Established in 1984, it carries over 15,000 gambling products that would make any Las Vegas lover swoon.

Originally located across the street, their new location, which opened in 2019, holds playing cards, lammers, dice, gaming tables, chip sets, dice sticks, and gambling memorabilia. A big draw of the store is the table-used card decks and dice from local casinos like the Golden Nugget, the Bellagio, and Caesars Palace. Because casinos change cards and dice frequently to guard against cheating, these table-used items are practically brand new, making for great gifts and souvenirs. There are also chips, ashtrays, and antique ads from bygone casinos for Vegas history lovers looking to add a bit of the real thing to your home casino.

The store also sells plenty of practical equipment like card shufflers and chip cases that can round out any at-home table-game collection. In the store's back room, you can browse slot machines, books, and displays telling the stories of local casinos and Las Vegas gambling history, or get some personalized chips. If you don't see what you're looking for in store, its huge website is sure to have just the thing.

But the store does more than sell souvenirs. During its four decades of operation, it has supplied chips to more casinos than any other chip maker in the world and remains a vital, but relatively unknown, part of Las Vegas gaming. The shop is also responsible for providing gambling supplies for screen use on well-known movies and shows like *The Sopranos*, *Casino*, *CSI*, *Ocean's Eleven* and *Rush Hour 2*.

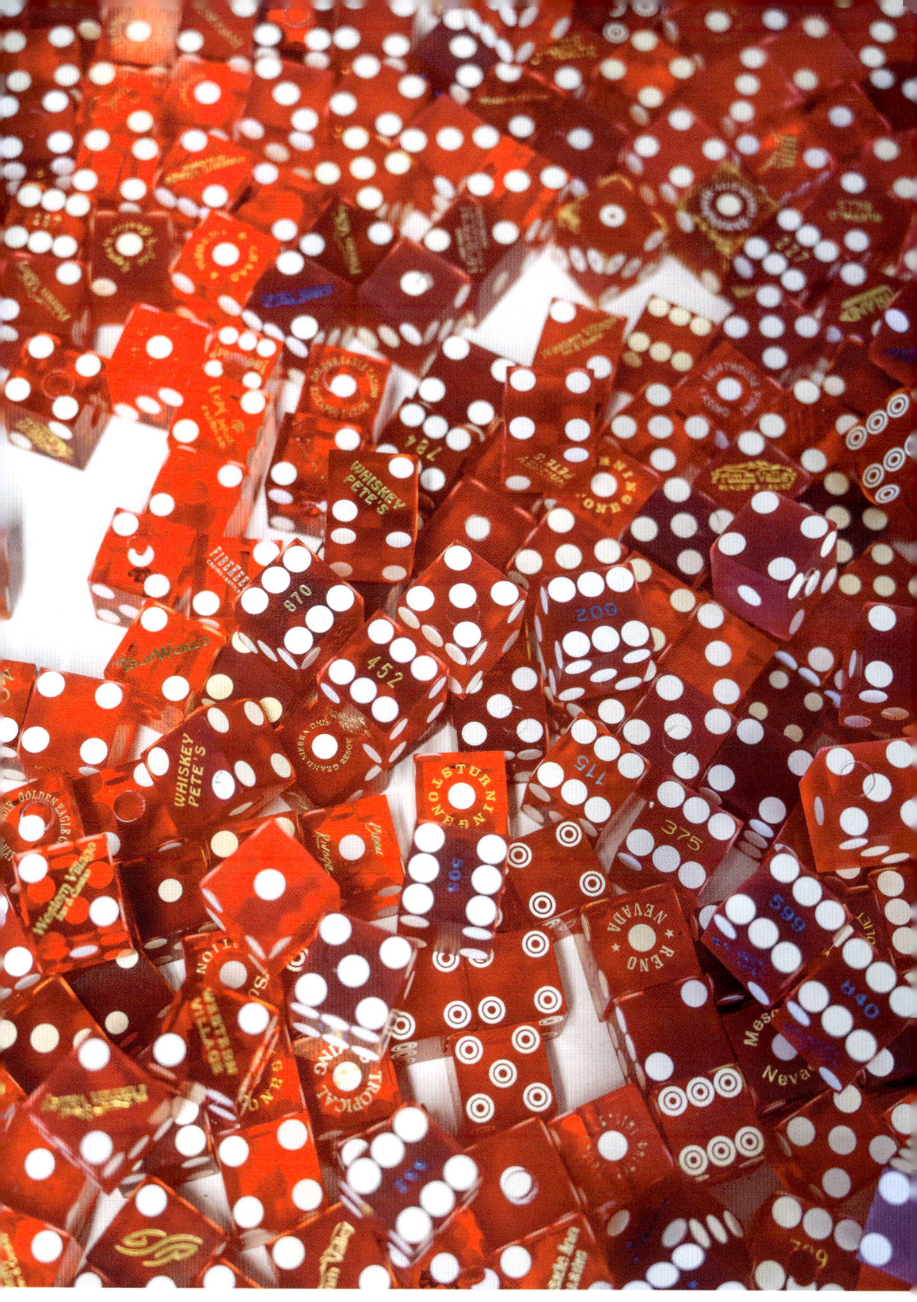

Address 727 South Main Street, Las Vegas, NV 89101, +1 (702) 382-9903, www.gamblersgeneralstore.com, info@ggslv.com | Getting there Deuce on the Strip Bus to Casino Center before Garces | Hours Mon–Sat 9am–5:30pm, Sun 9am–4:30pm | Tip For more Las Vegas memorabilia, check out the famous Gold & Silver Pawn Shop just down the street (713 Las Vegas Boulevard South, www.gspawn.com).

38 Garden Farms

Empowering locals to grow their own food

Because of the desert climate, urban sprawl, and massive wealth disparity, food deserts, or places with limited access to affordable and nutritious food, exist around the valley. These conditions often exist due to a lack of transport, access to stores, nutritious options, or low income. Garden Farms, a local urban farming nonprofit, has been able to close the gaps in the food deserts by having small local gardens in strategic areas and teaching desert-farming techniques to inspire individuals to create their own gardens.

Founder and CEO Bryan Vellinga and his wife Brittany started Garden Farms in 2010, first going to backyard residential gardens to help individuals grow in the harsh desert climate, gaining long-time customers year after year until it grew too large for the two of them. They brought on gardeners who were trained to grow food and teach others to do the same. They soon became involved with Clark County schools, installing gardens and sending out a farmer for regular lessons to teach children how to grow too. For more than a decade, their main goal has been to empower people to grow their own food. "Everything we do goes right back into our local community," says General Manager Wendy Wilson.

In 2017, they launched the Garden Farms Foundation to expand the school garden program to the now more than 100 school gardens, as well as to senior centers, rehabilitation centers, and apartment complexes, to teach people how to grow food in this climate and create better access to healthy foods.

Growing primarily vegetables, fruit trees, citrus-tree crops, berries, and grapes, they maintain two community farms, one in Pumpkin Park and one at Craig Ranch Regional Park, where they host regular community events like farmers markets, "pick your own" days, Farmer for a Day, the Green Thumb Academy, and community seed swaps to encourage small urban farmers and provide produce year round.

Address 405 Drake Street, Henderson, NV 89015, +1 (702) 551-4769, www.gardenfarms.net, info@gardenfarms.net | Getting there Bus 217 to Center after Ivy | Hours Mon–Fri 7am–3pm | Tip For more urban farming initiatives, visit Zion Urban Farm (2108 Revere Street, North Las Vegas, www.zionurbanfarm.org).

39 Gipsy Nightclub

Club at the center of Vegas' queer history

Local LGBTQ+ historian Dennis McBride proclaimed, "Nevada really is a wonderful place to be gay now." But it wasn't always that way. McBride, who has researched the state's gay history since the '70s, explained to *Las Vegas Weekly*, "Nevada's great area and small population kept queer people isolated," while state laws kept them "fearful and closeted." Even in the flamboyant neon-lit entertainment capital, the queer community thrived only at night, with bars and clubs becoming a haven for queer people to be themselves. McBride said, "The Las Vegas gay community first found its voice" at Le Café. While its run was short, owner Marge Jacques operated several other gay bars in Las Vegas before opening Gipsy. "It started with it being a place for the kids that didn't have a home, which is why it's called Gipsy," says Garrett Pattiani, marketing coordinator of the revived club. Gipsy could not advertise as a gay club because "homosexual activity" was still a felony, punishable by fines and prison, so advertising became coded. In an interview with the *Las Vegas Sun* in 1982, Marge said, "Everybody has a place to hang out… so that's why we started Gipsy for the show crowd," a euphemism for the queer community.

Over the next three decades, Gipsy sponsored Gay Pride celebrations, hosted the community's first AIDS benefit in November 1983, grew to be the state's largest employer of queer people, and drew in celebrities like Cher, Joan Rivers, Siegfried and Roy, Debbie Reynolds, and Liberace.

The original building was demolished in 2020 but was rebuilt in 2023 to host themed events and the popular drag brunch. Current owner Jerry Masini told *Chic Compass*, "The relaunch of Gipsy is a tribute to the LGBTQ+ community and Las Vegas nightlife. We are bringing back a sanctuary for performers and guests to express themselves freely in a space that respects our history and ushers in new entertainment experiences."

Address 4605 Paradise Road, Las Vegas, NV 89169, +1 (702) 731-1919, www.gipsylasvegas.com, info@gipsylasvegas.com | Getting there Bus 108 to Paradise after Naples or to University Center after Naples | Hours Check website for current hours and event details | Tip Head across the street to the sister bar, Piranha, for even more entertainment and LGBTQ+ events (4633 Paradise Road, www.piranhavegas.com).

40 Gold Strike Hot Springs

The hot spring oasis near the Hoover Dam

While hot springs occur in most of the western United States, Nevada is home to the highest concentration in the country. Though most are in the north, Southern Nevada has its fair share of this remarkable natural feature. Gold Strike Hot Springs is a group of natural hot springs along the Colorado River, just south of the Hoover Dam. While there's no proof of gold discovery in the area, the name may have come from the fact that the hot springs themselves were regarded with the same reverence as gold. Indigenous people in the southwest used hot springs for thousands of years, long before they were known to European settlers. The thermal springs provided warmth, healing mineral water, and cleansing.

The primitive soaking pools dotted along the canyon are fed by geothermally heated spring water that seeps out of the surrounding cliffs. The water emerges from the cliffs at around 109 degrees Fahrenheit while the pool water can range from 98 to 110 Fahrenheit. The hot springs can be accessed in two ways: by foot along the Goldstrike Canyon Trail or by kayak on the Colorado River. Both ways are challenging, with the canyon known for flash floods and extreme heat in the summer, along with eight tricky rope descents. The kayak trip often requires a few miles of paddling, depending on where you launch.

But reaching the hot springs makes the rigorous journey well worth it. The hot pools, hot waterfalls, and grottos that stretch along two miles of the canyon are said to be the best thing for sore muscles, minor skin ailments, pain and stress management, and even respiratory health. The often private and peaceful pools make for a perfect escape from the city and a chance to relax in nature, though experts are keen to relay that because temperatures can vary widely, it's important to not stay in the water too long, risking dehydration or overheating, especially important when you have a few-miles journey back.

Address Goldstrike Pass Road, Boulder City, NV 89005, +1 (702) 293-8990, www.nps.gov/lake | Getting there By car, take I-11 S to take exit 2 for US 93. Continue on Goldstrike Canyon Road for Goldstrike Canyon parking lot | Hours Oct–May dawn–dusk | Tip Continue the tour of the Colorado River with a kayak down to Emerald Cove, an inlet in the rock wall of emerald-green water (Willow Beach, Arizona, www.desert-adventures.com).

41 The Golden Tiki

An offbeat haunt in a Chinatown strip mall

Stepping inside The Golden Tiki is like being transported into the bygone era of excessive and kitschy Vegas, à la the Stardust's Aku Aku, featuring animal-print chairs, endless campy decor, and tropical-themed cocktails and delicacies. Opened in 2015, it's a local favorite, a frequent celebrity stop, and, according to bar staff and patrons, a haunted hotspot. Unexplainable anomalies like floating orbs, eerie shadows, and moving objects happen almost daily, some of which feature on an episode of *Ghost Adventures* with Las Vegas' Zak Bagans.

Many believe the artifacts are to blame for the spiritual activity, most notably the authentic headhunter machete and medicine-man bag, the skulls, and the various shrunken heads. Famous faces can be recognized on these heads, like famed Las Vegas Mayor Oscar Goodman, his wife (also Mayor Goodman), Walt Disney, Nicolas Cage, Evel Knievel, Ernest Hemingway, and Rob Zombie. Visitors will also notice three hula-girl dolls that dance above the bar, which were features of the It's a Small World attraction at Disneyland; a pregnant mummified mermaid; and, of course, the Golden Tiki idol.

The bar is themed around the story (which seems fit for the next *Pirates of the Caribbean* film) of the fictional William Tobias Faulkner, who terrorized the East Indies and the East India Company. The story goes that Captain Faulkner stole the Golden Tiki idol from Skull Island. He became entranced in the tiki's glowing red eyes and slowly drifted into madness, but not before scribbling his tale on the back of a nearby map.

Adam Rains, whose job title is chief mixologist, explorer, and worshipper of the tiki gods, is a gem, able to spout knowledge of the bar's history, story, and quirky patrons – and, of course, its haunted happenings. He makes a stop into the Golden Tiki worth it, even if the only spirits you're interested in are the liquid kind.

Address 3939 Spring Mountain Road, Las Vegas, NV 89102, +1 (702) 222-3196, www.thegoldentiki.com | Getting there Bus 203 to Spring Mountain after Valley View | Hours Open 24 hours | Tip For more tiki-bar action, drop into another local favorite, Frankie's Tiki Room (1712 W Charleston Boulevard, www.frankiestikiroom.com).

42 Grave of Yonema Tomiyasu

Resting place of pioneer horticulturist

Established in 1914, Woodlawn Cemetery is the oldest cemetery in Las Vegas. Gifted to the city by the San Pedro, Los Angeles, and Salt Lake Railroad, it has grown from 10 acres to its current 40 and is the final resting place for more than 20,000 citizens, including many prominent pioneers and notable locals. Among its many well-known graves, which include mobster Frank Cullotta (who inspired a character from the film *Casino*), William H. Briare (Mayor of Las Vegas from 1975–87), and "Diamondfield" Jack Davis (gunfighter and prospector), is that of Yonema "Bill" Tomiyasu.

Tomiyasu was a Japanese immigrant who relocated to California in 1898 before settling in Las Vegas. He bought the Passno property, just east of today's Sunset Park, and started growing alfalfa, an easy plant to grow in dry climates. He quickly became more skilled at farming the dry soil and was soon the leading supplier of peppers, lettuce, onions, carrots, melons, and beets for stores and restaurants throughout the city.

When work at the Hoover Dam began in the '30s, Tomiyasu supplied his produce to the Six Companies Inc., a store that provided food to the workers and their families in Boulder City. Soon after, Tomiyasu sold produce to the mess hall at the airplane gunnery school in Las Vegas (now Nellis Air Force Base).

Tomiyasu left a lasting legacy here in the valley: the Nevada Cooperative Extension Service still uses the plant calendar and plant list he created with his extensive research of desert-tolerant plant varieties and their optimal seasons; and the abundant fruitless mulberry trees that can be found around Las Vegas were introduced by Tomiyasu (his son, Nanyu, joked with the *Las Vegas Review-Journal* that allergy sufferers can thank his dad for their suffering). In his memory, Tomiyasu Lane near Sunset Park and Tomiyasu Elementary have also been named in his honor.

Address 1500 Las Vegas Boulevard North, Las Vegas, NV 89101, +1 (702) 229-6246, www.lasvegasnevada.gov/residents/parks-facilities/woodlawn-cemetery | Getting there Bus 113 to Las Vegas after Foremaster or Las Vegas before Foremaster | Hours Daily 5am–8pm | Tip Visit the graves of Pat Morita, known for playing Mr. Miyagi in *The Karate Kid*; local newspaper publisher Hank Greenspun; and actor Tony Curtis, at Palm Memorial Park (7600 S Eastern Avenue).

43 Harrison House

Visit a segregation-era guesthouse

When Las Vegas was coming into its entertainment era in the late 1930s and early '40s, it promoted many popular Black singers like Nat King Cole and Sammy Davis Jr., who drew massive crowds to resorts like the Sands and Flamingo. But this inclusion only lasted on the stage. Once performers were finished with their sets, segregation laws prohibited them from gambling, eating, or even sleeping at the resorts they were performing in. Black performers, though they brought in thousands of dollars for these casinos, were forced to find accommodation elsewhere. One such place was the Harrison Guest House.

Starting in 1942, Genevieve Harrison, a native of Texas, opened her home as a guesthouse to Black performers, as well as business people and divorcing couples who were barred from staying at white-only hotels. Dozens of big-name performers stayed in her home, including Pearl Bailey, Eddie "Rochester" Anderson, the Edwards Sisters, Arthur Lee Simpkins, Bob Parrish, and The Jubalaires, as well as Sammy Davis Jr., who stayed so frequently there is a room named after him.

Genevieve's home was featured in the 1949 edition of *The Green Book*, an annual guidebook for Black travelers that ran from 1936 to 1967 to help navigate Jim Crow laws to find lodging, businesses, and gas stations that would serve Black roadtrippers. Many similar guesthouses could be found across the US at this time, but after the Civil Rights Act of 1964, the need for them dwindled. The Harrison House is the last remaining example of a boarding house of this type in Las Vegas and possibly in all of Nevada. Because of this, it was listed in the National Register of Historic Places in 2016. "It's a symbol of resilience and community pride. It played a pivotal role in an affluent African American neighborhood that thrived despite the challenges of segregation."

Address 101 F Street, Las Vegas, NV 89106, +1 (702) 825-2145, www.harrisonhouselv.org, info@harrisonhouselv.org | Getting there Bus 208 to Washington after The D | Hours Open for scheduled tours only; reservation required | Tip View the nearby Historic Westside School, the oldest remaining school in Las Vegas, that started as the first school for Paiute children and then incorporated Black children who were unable to attend white schools (330 W Washington Avenue, www.lasvegasnevada.gov).

44 Helen J. Stewart Statue

Monument to the First Lady of Las Vegas

In 1882, Helen J. Stewart moved to Las Vegas after her husband, Archibald, had gained a parcel of land when Octavius Gass defaulted on his loan from the Stewarts. The family was only supposed to live on the land, which included the early Mormon settlement, for two years while they prepared to sell it. But on June 13, 1884, while Helen was pregnant with her fifth child, Archibald was killed by Schuyler Henry at Kiel Ranch during a gunfight (neither Henry nor Conrad Kiel were ever convicted of the murder).

Helen had no choice but to learn to operate a ranch on her land to care for her family. She not only provided for them, but she expanded the ranch, soon becoming the area's largest landowner. Her status in the town grew quickly, and in 1893, she became the first postmaster of Las Vegas (then called "Los" Vegas). In 1902, she sold her land to the San Pedro, Los Angeles, and Salt Lake Railroad, and in 1905 it became the city of Las Vegas.

Stewart continued her commitment to the city. She helped fund its first public library, assisted in forming the Las Vegas School District, and donated land to create the Las Vegas Grammar School, which, in 1923, was the first public school attended by Native American children from the Paiute colony. In 1916, she also served as the first female juror in Clark County. Helen was such an influential figure in the city that on the day of her funeral in 1926, all businesses closed for the day.

Her friend Delphine Squires bestowed her with the title of "First Lady of Las Vegas" and provided a fitting epitaph for Helen: "Her frail little body housed an indomitable will, a wonderful strength of purpose, and a courageous heart, and she faced death as she had faced the everyday problems of life with sublime fortitude."

The bronze statue of Helen, created by artist Benjamin Victor, is just outside the visitor center at the Old Ford Mormon State Park, on the land she first lived on when moving to the valley.

Address 500 E Washington Avenue, Las Vegas, NV 89101, +1 (702) 486-3511, parks.nv.gov/parks/old-las-vegas-mormon-fort | Getting there Bus 113 to Las Vegas at Cashman or Las Vegas before Cashman | Hours Tue–Sat 8am–4:30pm | Tip Pay a visit to the Nevada State Museum Las Vegas to learn more about the early settlers in the city, including the Native Americans, Mormon missionaries, and the Stewarts (309 S Valley View Boulevard, www.lasvegasnvmuseum.org).

45 High School Senior Squares

Student monument at the city's first high school

In the spring of 1941, Las Vegas High School senior Robbie Robinson pulled what might have been the first senior prank in the city. He and his friends painted a large "41" on the pavement in front of the school. When Principal Maude Frazier called the boys into her office, they denied their involvement, though the paint on their shoes gave them away. Frazier saw the prank as an opportunity to boost school spirit and class pride, thus the Senior Squares tradition began, or so one story goes.

The tradition officially started with the class of 1946 (some attribute the gap of '42–'45 to small class sizes when many young men were sent overseas during WWII) and continued until 1988. The squares were a serious tradition at this time, with students treating them with reverence (you weren't supposed to step on the squares). Despite many attempts to seal and preserve them, they eventually fell into disrepair. In 2013, the designs were recreated on smaller tiles and placed in the monument to preserve their legacy. Rollie Gibbs, class of '54 and then president of the alumni association, raised $50,000 for building materials that were then constructed by alumni volunteers or their friends.

The squares are like a time capsule, with most designs tied into that year's yearbook or events. Designs range from an atomic bomb blast from the class of '51 to a carrot and bone for the class of '73 (apparently an inside joke about the football team). But the significance of the squares goes beyond the students. For decades, this was the only high school in all of Las Vegas. The entire community was connected to the school with everyone coming out to games and school events, and celebrating the graduations of the city's highest academic level. The legacy of the squares, says current alumni president and historian Joe Thomson, is "the history of the entire city, not just the high school."

Address 315 S 7th Street, Las Vegas, NV 89101 | **Getting there** Deuce on the Strip Bus to 4th at Fremont Street Experience | **Hours** Unrestricted | **Tip** Check out the nearby Historic Fifth Street School, which is on the National Register of Historic Places (401 S 4th Street, www.lasvegasnevada.gov).

46 Historic Railroad Trail

Hike to the Hoover Dam

During construction of the Hoover Dam in the early 1930s, trains transported supplies to the remote worksite. Six Companies, Inc. built nearly 30 miles of railroad to connect Boulder City to the cement mixing plants, quarry pits, and gravel-sorting plants around Clark County. A US Government line also transported materials staged and constructed in Boulder City to the dam. Running 24 hours a day, these trains were an integral part of completing the dam, transporting tons of supplies in a relatively quick and efficient way.

To get to the worksite, five massive tunnels were cut into the rock, each about 25 feet wide, 30 feet high, and 300 feet long, to accommodate the large pieces fabricated in Boulder City. These tracks were managed and operated by the Bureau of Reclamation until 1963 when the dam's power-generating facility was completed. While these tracks were dismantled shortly after, the area is now home to the Historic Railroad Trail, a National Historic Trail. The trail runs from Lakeshore Road near the Lake Mead Visitor Center all the way to the Hoover Dam, making it a really special and unique way to visit.

Because of the wide, flat path carved into the landscape to accommodate the trains and massive cargo, it makes for an easy hike or bike for people of all experiences and fitness levels. The 3.7-mile trail takes you through five tunnels, gives additional information on the train lines and construction of the dam, and offers amazing views of Lake Mead and the surrounding mountains that you can't get anywhere else.

Close to the dam is a "boneyard" with archeological remnants of the original equipment used to build it. This is one of the few opportunities to view the equipment used in the dam's construction because much of the evidence was taken away or now lies at the bottom of Lake Mead, which was created after the dam's completion.

Address Historic Railroad Trail Access, Lakeshore Road, Boulder City, NV 89005, +1 (702) 293-8990, www.nps.gov/lake | Getting there By car, take I-11 to Boulder City, turn onto Boulder City Parkway, then turn onto Lakeshore Road to find the trailhead parking lot | Hours Daily dawn–dusk | Tip Continue your railroad tour with a visit to the Nevada State Railroad Museum to learn about local railroad history (601 Yucca Street, Boulder, www.boulderrailroadmuseum.org).

47 Historic Westside Legacy Park

Park dedicated to Black History and the Westside

The Historic Westside Legacy Park is a stunning design project honoring the past, present, and future leaders of West Las Vegas. Opened in 2021, the park itself is a quiet place of respite among the hustle and bustle of the city. A place to reflect, learn, and dream, visitors can find out all about the Westside and its inhabitants. As a primarily Black neighborhood that came into being during segregation laws and racism throughout the city, this area is often overlooked when it comes to the history of Las Vegas.

The park includes public art, a reflective walking path, a children's play area, and an event plaza that displays a map of the historic Westside neighborhood. This outdoor museum aims to accurately and respectfully tell the story of how the community started and has evolved.

Chase McCurdy, a local artist from the Westside, was brought in to advise on the cultural elements but also to create sculptures. His installation, called *Living Black Pillars*, comprises polished stainless steel orbs, symbolizing the foundation laid by ancestors that have enabled the next generations to reach new heights.

To tell the story of this notable community, the design firm LGA Architecture has incorporated local honorees who have made significant contributions to the community through activism, philanthropy, outreach, education, and cultural merit.

Among the honorees are such community leaders as Huedillard "H.P." Fitzgerald, the first African American man to graduate from the University of Nevada, Reno, and the first African American school principal in Nevada; James Gay III, the first African American to work in an executive capacity of a major casino; and Dr. Esther Langston, the first African American social worker in the state of Nevada, and the first African American woman employed at UNLV.

Address 1600 Mount Mariah Drive, Las Vegas, NV 89106, +1 (702) 229-6011, www.lasvegasnevada.gov | Getting there Bus 105 to Martin L. King after Jimmy | Hours Daily 7am–11pm | Tip Drive down Jackson Avenue, once known as the Black Strip, which was home to casinos during the '50s and '60s, when segregation made it impossible for Black citizens to visit white-only casinos on Fremont.

48 Hotel Apache

Fremont's famed haunted hotel

With only 81 rooms, no spa, or large theater, Hotel Apache is tiny by Vegas standards. But it was once considered the pinnacle of luxury, with air conditioning, electric elevators, private bathrooms, and automatic locks that were on par with hotels in New York or Chicago, and decades ahead of those in Vegas. Opened in 1932 by Pietro Ottavio Silvagni, it drew notable celebrity visitors like Humphrey Bogart, Lucille Ball, and Clark Gable, and is also said to be the casino that made poker a mainstream game.

The hotel was acquired by infamous casino tycoon Benny Binion in 1951. Though it changed hands a few times and closed in 2009 due to the recession, it reopened in 2019 under the Binions' conglomerate, owned by TLC Casino Enterprises, Inc. Despite its early glamor, there have been hundreds of reports of ghostly encounters. Guests report hearing voices, seeing objects move, seeing shadows, hearing sounds of shuffling paper, lights turning on and off, and feeling as if they are not alone.

Elizabeth Bristow, Social Media Manager for TLC Casinos, told KTNV she stayed in the hotel before opening as a test run. She began to hear noises in the next room as if someone was moving furniture and trying to open the newly sealed windows. She became concerned that the person next door would accidentally break something. "So I called down to our front desk. She goes, 'Hold on for a second. There's no one in that room.'"

Reportedly, the most haunted room is Room 400, the penthouse, but almost every room on the property has had at least one story, causing the hotel to quickly gain a reputation as a haunted hotspot. Vegas' own Zak Bagans and his team visited the hotel in a 2019 episode of their show *Ghost Adventures*, experiencing phenomena they claim prove the hauntings. Whether searching for ghosts or looking to experience a piece of old Vegas history, Hotel Apache can be a great escape.

Address 128 E Fremont Street, Las Vegas, NV 89101, +1 (702) 382-1600, www.binions.com, reservations@binions.com | Getting there Deuce on the Strip Bus to Fremont Street Experience (Carson after Casino Center or Carson at Third) | Hours Unrestricted | Tip For more spooky encounters, visit the most popular haunted attraction in the city, Zak Bagans' Haunted Museum (600 E Charleston, www.thehauntedmuseum.com).

49 Huntridge Theater

Legendary theater brought back to life

The Huntridge Theater, the gem of the historic Huntridge neighborhood, is one of the city's most iconic landmarks due to its long history and beautiful Art Deco design. Opened in 1944, it was designed by renowned architect S. Charles Lee, known for the Fox Wilshire Theatre (now the Saban Theatre in Beverly Hills) and the Hollywood Melrose Hotel (now Hollywood Historic Hotel). The Art Deco design of the Huntridge uses curved lines mixed with bold geometric shapes to give it a futuristic look for that era, while its distinctive marquee, topped with its neon sign, draws the eye from anywhere in the neighborhood.

In the 1950s and '60s, the theater, then a cinema, was a popular spot to see the latest Hollywood releases. Elvis is even said to have rented it for private viewings. By the '80s, a shift in entertainment trends made it difficult for the Huntridge to compete, transitioning into a live events venue in 1992. Unfortunately, because the building had been constructed during WWII, when steel was hard to come by outside of the war effort, the roof trusses for the grand building were made with Douglas Fir pine. In July 1995, after the wood had been baking in the Vegas heat for 50 years, the roof collapsed just as the punk rock group the Circle Jerks were set to perform. The nonprofit Friends of the Huntridge Theater fixed the structure and held shows for renowned performers like the Red Hot Chili Peppers, The Killers, Foo Fighters, No Doubt, the Beastie Boys, and Sublime. And though it gained a spot on the National Register of Historic Places in 1993, it eventually closed in 2004. The property was then purchased by real estate developer J Dapper in 2021. The new Huntridge will feature live music, off-Broadway productions, and artistic events that will "educate and strengthen the Las Vegas community and culture," the company says. The iconic neon sign was relit in 2023 with over 1,000 people watching, bringing it a step closer to returning to its former glory.

Address 1208 E Charleston Boulevard, Las Vegas, NV 89104, +1 (702) 733-3622, www.thehuntridge.com, theater@dapperdevelopment.com | Getting there Bus 206 to Charleston after Maryland | Hours Currently viewable from the outside only | Tip See more Art Deco-inspired architecture (and amazing concerts and shows) at the renowned Smith Center for the Performing Arts (361 Symphony Park Avenue, www.thesmithcenter.com).

50_Il Toro E La Capra

Mexican-Italian fusion

Il Toro E La Capra is a one-of-a-kind fusion of Mexican and Italian cuisines. Opened in January 2022, it's the latest venture from Javier Barajas, the visionary behind the Lindo Michoacan restaurant group. Barajas, who emigrated from Michoacán, Mexico in the 1970s, drew inspiration from his lifelong love of both Mexican and Italian cuisine. He learned to cook Mexican food from his mother and honed his Italian skills with nuns at his high school in Michoacán. "It was my dream to create a Mexican-Italian fusion restaurant," Barajas said, noting the shared ingredients and deep cultural roots of both cuisines.

The restaurant's name is deeply personal, honoring Barajas' youngest children. Capra, meaning goat, "comes from my daughter. She used to climb everywhere, even on the fridge!" said Barajas. "Toro comes from my son. He looks like a bull I had in Mexico."

Barajas and his son Leo, a chef at the restaurant, lead menu creation, drawing on travel, family, and tradition. "When I travel, I love to go to different restaurants and get new ideas and inspiration from personal experiences in order to add a lot of depth to the dishes," Barajas said. The seafood-rich Marco Polo I Soup and Steak Tampiqueña reflect his personal tastes. The Carnitas y Chicharron Pizza and Pasta Azteca are both delicious marriages of the two cuisines. A standout dish is the Pasta Sarandeada Javier Cresencio, named after Barajas' late son. "He was supposed to be working here. Thinking of him makes us work even harder."

Inside, vintage rustic decor, Italian antiques, and hand-painted murals evoke a nostalgic yet warm atmosphere. "I wanted people to feel at home and like they can have kids and be loud… Our restaurant is the complete opposite of those very serious Italian spots," Barajas explained. "This is the best restaurant in Las Vegas – even if people don't know it yet."

Address 6435 S Decatur Boulevard, Las Vegas, NV 89118, +1 (702) 331-6090, www.toroelacapra.com, iltoroelacapra@iltoroelacapra.com | Getting there Bus 212 or 103 to Decatur after Sunset | Hours Mon–Thu 11am–10pm, Fri 11am–11pm, Sat 10am–11pm, Sun 10am–10pm | Tip Visit the well-known sister restaurant Lindo Michoacan at the original location for regional Mexican food in a family atmosphere (2655 E Desert Inn Road, lindomichoacan.com).

51 International Theater at The Westgate

Elvis' most famous venue in Vegas

Perhaps no one is more associated with Vegas than Elvis Presley. Beyond the Rat Pack and the mobsters, Elvis is an unofficial mascot of the city. Though his start here was lackluster (his first shows at The New Frontier in 1956 were not a hit), he loved Vegas, specifically the other performers like Liberace and Paul Anka. After finding success on *The Milton Berle Show* with his rendition of "Hound Dog" and later his performance in the movie *Viva Las Vegas,* he returned for a show at the International Hotel (now the Westgate) in 1969. The show was an instant success. "He hadn't done a concert in nine years, and he came out that night inside this historical theater, and man, that was it," his stepbrother, David Stanley, told *Las Vegas Magazine*. "I thought 'My god, this guy!' I went up to him and said, 'Elvis, that was unbelievable.' And he said, 'David, I've been wrong for so long, but I was right tonight.'"

Elvis went on to perform two shows a night for 30 days straight, two months of the year. He sold out a consecutive 636 shows between '69 and '76.

While fans of The King can feel his presence almost everywhere in the city, one place to get a real feel for him is, of course, at the Westgate. As *Travel Weekly* put it, "Elvis Lives… All Year at the Westgate." From the life-sized statue of Elvis in the lobby to the memorabilia case, you never forget the Westgate's connection to the singer. But the place connected more so than any other property is the International Theater, where he performed his hit shows. The over-1,600-seat venue has seen performances by Liberace, Wayne Newton, Barbara Streisand, and more recently Barry Manilow, but the legacy of Elvis will never leave it. "He left so much of his soul on that stage," Stanley recalled. "He gave so much of himself. Elvis left a mark."

Address 3000 Paradise Road, Las Vegas, NV 89109, +1 (702) 732-5111, www.westgateresorts.com | Getting there Bus 108 to Paradise after Elvis Presley or Paradise after Convention Center | Hours Check website for event schedule | Tip Continue learning about Elvis on a backstage tour with David Stanley on his monthly "My Brother Elvis" tours (www.westgate.com).

52_Jean-Marie Auboine Chocolatier

High-end French chocolates with a twist

World-renowned Master Chocolatier Jean-Marie Auboine is among the top chocolatiers in the country, if not the world. With experience working in top-rated restaurants in France, Switzerland, and Monaco, as the Executive Pastry Chef at Fontainebleau Miami Beach hotel and Bellagio, Jean-Marie founded his company in 2011, supplying hand-crafted confections to luxury resorts like The Ritz-Carlton, Four Seasons, and Waldorf Astoria (plus most hotels on the Strip). Luckily, you don't have to stay at one of these resorts to try his award-winning chocolates. The showroom on Harmon Avenue is packed with chocolate bars, caramels, hot chocolate powders, and spreads, while huge refrigerated display cases are lined with exquisitely decorated chocolates and macarons, ready for sampling.

The vibrant colors, glossy exteriors, and uncommon shapes of the chocolates are a departure from the traditional French style and are little works of art. Chef Auboine keeps the French technique, using premium ingredients (the Swiss-made chocolate is exclusive to his business), and elevating it with colorful designs, beautiful shapes, and innovative flavors to create a beautiful blend of French and American aesthetics. Some surprising flavors include the "Passione," a passion-fruit and caramel with milk chocolate confection in a yellow-orange truncated pyramid, and their "Elysee," a speckled blue dome with honey saffron ganache in milk chocolate.

Executive Vice President Chanelle Bautista equated the showroom to a wine tasting, where sampling is encouraged and helps broaden the mind to new flavors and textures. It's the perfect way to spend an afternoon, not just for the treats, but for the chance to connect with the warm, knowledgeable staff who are as passionate about their craft as they are about welcoming their visitors.

Address 4780 W Harmon Avenue, Suite 1, Las Vegas, NV 89103, +1 (702) 222-0535, www.jmauboinechocolates.com | Getting there Bus 103 to Decatur after Harmon or Decatur before Harmon | Hours Mon–Fri 9am–5pm | Tip For another chocolate experience, try out Ethel M Chocolate Factory & Cactus Garden (2 Cactus Garden Drive, www.ethelm.com).

53 Kaqun Wellness Spa

One-of-a-kind wellness experience

While Las Vegas is known for some impressive and luxurious day spas, Kaqun Wellness Spa is something entirely different. It's a revolutionary wellness experience based on oxygen therapy, frequented by local professional athletes, performers, and those seeking deep healing. The story of Kaqun began in 2002 in the Visegrád Mountains of Hungary. Dr. Robert Lyons, Ph.D., O.MD, set out to create a product capable of delivering oxygen in a completely new way. After years of research and clinical testing with accredited universities and government institutions, the Kaqun water system was born – a scientifically advanced method to stabilize oxygen in water, designed to help combat hypoxia (low oxygen in the cells), boost energy, and detox from within.

The Las Vegas location, which opened in 2015, has its own powerful story. Director Aniko Brown was diagnosed with stage 4 pancreatic cancer at 19 years old. While undergoing conventional treatment, she returned to her native Hungary to undergo Kaqun Water Therapy. After consistent sessions over months, her tumor shrank enough for doctors at UCLA to operate. Today, Aniko is cancer-free and dedicated to sharing this therapy with others.

Kaqun offers treatments like the 50-minute oxygen-absorbing water-therapy sessions, infrared sauna blanket therapy, and a hyperbaric oxygen chamber in elegant, private spa rooms. These treatments increase cellular oxygen levels, promote detoxification, and have shown benefits like reduced chemo side effects, faster wound healing, improved athletic recovery, and powerful anti-aging effects.

With a commitment to healing and innovation, Kaqun Wellness Spa continues to lead the way in oxygen-based therapies, providing an oasis of health, vitality, and hope in the heart of Las Vegas. Those experiencing an illness, stress, physical pain – or who are just in need of a relaxing soak – must visit Kaqun.

Address 8330 S Rainbow Boulevard, Las Vegas, NV 89139, +1 (702) 586-7751, www.kaqunlv.com | Getting there Bus 101 to Rainbow before Shelbourne or Rainbow after Shelbourne | Hours Mon–Fri 8am–4pm, Sat & Sun 8am–1:30pm | Tip For a more traditional spa experience, indulge in the top-ranked Aria Spa & Salon (3730 Las Vegas Boulevard South, aria.mgmresorts.com).

54 Kiel Ranch

One of the earliest ranches in the valley

Kiel Ranch (sometimes spelled Kyle) was one of the earliest ranches established in the Las Vegas Valley. Conrad Kiel acquired the land in 1875, and it is the area thought to have been where Mormon missionaries attempted to teach Native Americans in the 1850s. The adobe building on the property is believed to date from this Mormon period. The area contained one of the oldest natural springs in Nevada, an important water source for the Native tribes and later the settlers on the land. Kiel established a 250-acre ranch that produced hay, fruits, and vegetables that fed miners and early settlers.

It is also the site of a well-known murder during the early days of Las Vegas. Rival rancher Archibald Stewart (husband of Helen J. Stewart) was murdered on the ranch in 1884. Though neither Kiel nor his accomplices were found guilty, it was widely known that Kiel was responsible. In fact, Kiel's two sons were found dead in 1900, which many people believe was retribution by Stewart's own sons.

In 1903, a portion of the land was sold to William A. Clark to build the San Pedro, Los Angeles, and Salt Lake Railroad. The rest of the land was bought in 1911 by banker John S. Park, who built a home, the "White House," on the land. It remained here until it was destroyed by fire in 1992.

Today, the springs and buildings are preserved on the seven-acre Kiel Ranch Historic Park. The structures include a cottage called the Doll House, one of the oldest standing adobe structures in Nevada, and a brick commissary. The historic structures are along walking paths dotted with informational signs and shaded picnic areas, making for a small oasis in the middle of an industrial area.

The park underwent restoration in 2024 to restore the buildings and revive one of the oldest orchards in Southern Nevada. The restoration project will provide educational resources while also increasing public access to fresh food.

Address 2465 Kiel Way, Las Vegas, NV 89030, +1 (702) 633-2418, www.cityofnorthlasvegas.com | Getting there Bus 214 to Carey after Englestad | Hours Daily 6am–11pm | Tip Visit the abandoned Binion House, home of former Horseshoe Club Owner Benny Binion (2400 West Bonanza Road).

55 Las Vegas Circus Center

Learn from Vegas' best performers

The spectacular Cirque du Soleil shows are some of the most sought-after performances in Vegas. While *O* at the Bellagio, *Michael Jackson ONE* at Mandalay Bay, and *KÀ* at the MGM Grand captivate audiences with gravity-defying stunts, just west of the Strip is the Las Vegas Circus Center, a hub where many of these performers train and nurture the next generation of circus talent.

Opened in December 2018, LVCC is a place where professionals can train and rehearse on high-quality equipment while students can learn from and be inspired by professionals. Many of the instructors are professionals who work on the Strip or have retired from multi-generational circus families. Such professionals include: trampwall coach, two-time French Olympian, and artist from *Michael Jackson ONE* Greg Pennes; *Mystère* power track tumbler Grisha Alkov; and Bruno Vargas, member of the flying family that toured with many renowned circus acts, such as Ringling Bros.

LVCC has quickly become a mecca for the circus community, with people visiting from all over the world to learn new skills or be around some of the top performers in the game. The environment at LVCC is positive and supportive, a place where people walk in with a smile and spend hours catching up with friends between classes. The center has helped foster young performers, many of them growing into professionals.

The facilities feature a flying trapeze, multiple trampolines, a power track, an air track, two large spring floors, a marley floor, multiple aerial apparatus, slackwire, and a ninja course, among other specialty gear and tools. The equipment is extensive enough that they regularly host auditions for some of the biggest names in the entertainment industry. Even if you're not a professional, many of the classes can be taken by beginners to learn new skills and have fun, like the popular flying trapeze and trampwall/trampoline.

Address 6425 S Jones Boulevard, #102, Las Vegas, NV 89118, +1 (833) 324-7287, www.lasvegascircuscenter.com, info@lasvegascircuscenter.com | Getting there Bus 102 to Jones after Sunset | Hours Check website for class schedule | Tip For another Vegas-only experience, try your hand at exotic car racing at Speed Vegas (14200 Las Vegas Boulevard South, www.speedvegas.com).

56_The Las Vegas Farm

Sanctuary giving animals a second chance at life

Just off Grand Teton Drive near Silverado Ranch is an animal sanctuary housing peacocks, cats, dogs, pigs, sheep, chickens, goats, cows, fish, turtles, llamas, and horses. The farm has been rehabilitating and protecting local animals since 1961. Led by owner Sharon Linsenbardt since the very beginning, it is run completely by volunteers, including Linsenbardt (who has never taken a paycheck), whose love for the animals is unmistakable. The farm consists of The Market, an open-air shop selling everything from eggs and honey (sourced from their chickens and 124 beehives) to T-shirts and books; the White Peacock wedding chapel (a gorgeous wooden chapel perfect for rustic, nature-loving couples); and the Barn Buddies Sanctuary, which is home to their animals. Proceeds from the market and entrance fees to the sanctuary all go back to the animals for their food, medical needs, shelter, and care.

All animals that arrive on the farm are vaccinated, neutered or spayed, and brought back to full health. Many of the animals come to the sanctuary because they have been either severely neglected or abused, meaning they need extensive medical care, like Backy, a black and white Apple Gelding horse who needed over $15,000 in surgeries after arriving with severe injuries to his head and face. But Linsenbardt doesn't regret spending that kind of money on the animals. She says they deserve the opportunity to live and she will do everything in her power to make that happen. All animals are cared for at the farm for the rest of their natural lives, never adopted out or put down, which many critics suggest.

But Linsenbardt says the answer is not to put down the animals, but to stop unnecessary breeding and buying of animals people can't care for, like 400-pound pig Homer who previously lived in a residential home. Until that happens, Sharon and her team of volunteers will do what they can for the animals under their care.

Address 7222 W Grand Teton Drive, Las Vegas, NV 89131, +1 (702) 982-8000, www.thelasvegasfarm.com, contact@thelasvegasfarm.com | Getting there Bus 106 to Farm after Buffalo | Hours Sat & Sun 9am–4pm, weekdays by appointment | Tip For larger, less native animals, visit Lion Habitat Ranch (382 Bruner Avenue, Henderson, www.lionhabitatranch.org).

57_Las Vegas Mannequins

Free "museum" of shop mannequins

Tucked away in an industrial area of Las Vegas is one of the city's most unusual and fascinating hidden spots: the Las Vegas Mannequins warehouse. This 23,000-square-foot space doubles as a quirky, ever-changing "museum" that the *Reno Gazette Journal* called "a wonderland of inanimate characters from eras old and new." Visitors can freely explore a surreal landscape of mannequins posed in dramatic, bizarre, and sometimes humorous ways.

Founded in 2004 by Alison Wainwright, Las Vegas Mannequins began as a small, part-time venture out of her garage, renting mannequins for trade shows and events to display clothes and costumes. Today, it has grown into one of the top suppliers of mannequins and store fixtures in the US and Canada with clientele ranging from high-end retail outfits to walk-ins looking for pieces to display items for their online shop.

But the showroom remains a passion project that reflects Wainwright's creative spirit. It feels more like an avant-garde art installation in the middle of uncanny valley than a retail operation. Mannequins of every shape, size, and style – from classic fashion forms to hyper-stylized and futuristic figures – are arranged in rotating displays. Some are dressed in striking clothes, while most are bold and bare, holding a variety of poses. The mannequins also range from realistic forms in natural skin tones and painted-on faces to others with missing limbs and faces in bold, bright colors.

While the main business of Las Vegas Mannequins is to provide mannequins, displays, and store fixtures to companies across North America, the showroom experience, free to the public and unlike anything in town, makes it a truly strange and delightful piece of Vegas culture. Even those uninterested in mannequins or the retail business will find this free art installation interesting, unusual, and mesmerizing.

Address 3900 W Desert Inn Road, Las Vegas, NV 89102, +1 (702) 987-5830, www.lvmannequins.com | Getting there Bus 104 to Valley View after Desert Inn or Valley View before Desert Inn | Hours Mon–Fri 9am–4pm | Tip Explore another quirky museum, the world-famous Omega Mark at Meow Wolf with interactive and mind-bending displays (3215 Rancho Drive #100).

58 Liberace Garage

Extravagant cars from the famed performer

Inside the Hollywood Cars Museum is the Liberace Garage, a venue dedicated to showcasing the extravagant automotive collection of the legendary entertainer. This exceptional display offers visitors a glimpse into the opulent lifestyle of one of Vegas' most iconic performers.

Władziu Valentino Liberace, known only as Liberace, was a Polish-American pianist, singer, and actor celebrated for his flamboyant performances and lavish lifestyle. He made his first appearance in Las Vegas in 1944, well before the Rat Pack or Elvis, and by the '50s, he had become a mainstay on the Strip. His performance at the Las Vegas Hilton drew large audiences, and his penchant for luxury extended beyond the stage, influencing the city's culture and entertainment scene. Liberace made showbiz history in 1958 when he became the first performer to drive a car onto a stage during a live show. This innovative move blended his love for luxury with his theatrical flair, setting a new standard for live entertainment.

The Liberace Foundation, which manages the artifacts from Liberace's decades in entertainment, oversees the garage, giving visitors a chance to see these unforgettable vehicles up close. The most renowned cars include the 1961 Rolls-Royce Phantom V, which was used for his grand entrances at the Las Vegas Hilton (it also featured in the 2013 biopic *Behind the Candelabra)* and the crystal-covered roadster in which he arrived on stage at New York's Radio City Music Hall. Among the cars are rotating exhibits of some of Liberace's costumes and stage props, including three stage-used pianos, one of which was played at the 2019 Grammys. The Liberace Garage is a window into the extravagant world of Liberace, showcasing not only his vehicles but also reflecting the broader cultural impact of his performances and style, proving he was truly a tour de force in the world of showbiz.

Address 5115 Dean Martin Drive, Unit 905, Las Vegas, NV 89118, +1 (702) 330-4225, www.hollywoodcarsmuseum.com | Getting there Bus 119 to Reno after Las Vegas or Bus 104 to Valley View after Reno | Hours Daily 10am–5pm | Tip Get a glimpse of one of Liberace's properties at the illustrious Liberace Mansion (4982 Shirley Street, www.theliberacemansion.com).

59 Little Church of the West

Say "I do" at Elvis' Viva Las Vegas wedding chapel

Opened in 1943, the Little Church of the West is one of the first wedding chapels in Vegas and among the longest-operating businesses in the city. First located on the North Strip as part of the New Frontier Hotel, it moved three times over the years until, in 1996, it found its current home on South Las Vegas Boulevard near the famous "Welcome to Las Vegas" sign.

While the location has changed, the building itself is the original, having been moved all in one piece about two-tenths of a mile south. Architect and builder William J. Moore Jr. designed it in the style of a typical pioneer church to tie in with the New Frontier's Old West decor. The exterior is made from cedar, while the interior is California redwood, which makes the space feel warm and intimate. The chapel's Victorian lamps are thought to be from 19th-century railroad cars that have been converted to electric. "It hasn't changed," said current owner, Greg Smith. "There's been some painting and re-carpeting, but the pews in there are believed to be the ones built with the chapel in 1942."

The chapel is most well known for being in the iconic *Viva Las Vegas* film, where Elvis marries Ann-Margret's character. While Elvis didn't actually get hitched here (that was at the Aladdin Hotel, where Planet Hollywood is now), many real-life celebrities found themselves saying "I do" in the little church. Famous couples include Betty Grable and Harry James, Zsa Zsa Gabor and George Sanders, Judy Garland and Mark Herron, Richard Gere and Cindy Crawford, and Billy Bob Thornton and Angelina Jolie.

But they're not alone: over 250,000 couples have been hitched at the Little Church of the West, the only building on the Strip on the National Register of Historic Places. With the church's colorful past and cozy atmosphere, it's easy to see why so many choose this little chapel over the more than 50 on the Las Vegas Strip alone.

Address 4617 Las Vegas Boulevard South, Las Vegas, NV 89119, +1 (702) 739-7971, www.littlechurchofthewest.com, info@littlechurchlv.com | Getting there Deuce on the Strip Bus to the Welcome to Las Vegas Sign | Hours Daily 8am–11pm | Tip Check out Graceland Wedding Chapel, known as the first chapel with an Elvis theme and impersonator. It featured in the films *Fear and Loathing in Las Vegas* and *Fools Rush In* (619 Las Vegas Boulevard South, www.gracelandchapel.com).

60 Luv-It Frozen Custard

Hand-crafted frozen custard since 1973

Luv-It Frozen Custard, found on East Oakey near the Arts District, has been a Las Vegas institution since 1973. In the original building and location, it has been run by the same family for four generations now, a veritable unicorn in Vegas. Managed by Sharon and her son Brandon (the fourth generation), it remains a staple of the community; a favorite place to grab a cold treat, especially on hot summer days. In fact, former Mayor Caroline Goodman gave them the Keys to the City in 2021 to recognize their long history and commitment to the city.

Many return to Luv-It time and again for nostalgia, but also for the quality of its products. Frozen custard, ice cream's thicker and more decadent cousin, is made with egg yolks along with cream and sweetener. Luv-It's custard is made fresh daily with as many local ingredients as possible. Many of the toppings are also made in-house, like the buttered roasted salted pecans, which is made in 30- to 60-pound batches each week.

While there are 34 flavors in the collection, only four are offered each day: chocolate, vanilla, and two unique rotating flavors, including champagne, cherry, fresh banana nut, Sin-a-Buns, and apple spice, to name a few. One of the newer flavors is Blue Moon, a vibrant neon-blue-colored almond custard. These flavors can be made into sundaes, shakes, malts, or quarts to go. Luv-It's monthly schedule is found on its website and mobile app, but if you've got a craving for one not listed, shakes and malts can be made from any that are offered. A must-try is the Western Sundae with hot fudge, caramel, and the signature pecans, but with over 55 types of sundaes, it's hard to choose the best one.

While the stand may not look like much, consisting of a walk-up window (no seating inside or out), there is plenty of free parking and a backdrop of the Strat Hotel, which makes for some pretty cool Instagram pictures.

Address 505 E Oakey Boulevard, Las Vegas, NV 89104, +1 (702) 384-6452, www.luvitfrozencustard.com | **Getting there** Deuce on the Strip Bus to NB Las Vegas before Oakey or SB at Oakey | **Hours** Sun–Thu 1–10pm, Fri & Sat 1–11pm | **Tip** For another downtown shop, try Dig It! Coffee Co., a local coffee house that provides employment for adults of all abilities (1300 S Casino Center Boulevard #110, www.digitcoffeeco.com).

61 Mermaid Swimmers

Real mermaids in the middle of the desert

Mermaids may be mythical, but mermaiding – an enchanting water ballet performed by divers and synchronized swimmers – is very much real. The most popular place to see them in Southern Nevada is at the rustic lodge-style Silverton Casino just south of the Strip. Billed as the "Best Free Attraction in Las Vegas," this family-friendly show features swimmers dressed as mermaids, "dancing" in a 117,000-gallon aquarium. The performers effortlessly glide, twist, and twirl through the water among the more than 1,500 fish, including sharks and stingrays.

The Silverton Aquarium first opened in 2004 with a show called *Azure*. Similar to a Cirque show, it featured underwater performers and divers, some of which were mermaids. After the show ended, the mermaids remained, becoming the wildly popular attraction they are today.

All the mermaids are SCUBA certified, says Kristin Janise, Silverton's Aquatics Safety Manager and PADI-certified Mermaid Instructor, ensuring they can safely perform underwater using hookah lines, which are long hoses that deliver compressed air to divers. All the hard work that goes into the performances to make them safe and look effortless is worth it to "spread a little bit of magic and joy, and see the kids' faces light up when they get to see a real mermaid," Janise says.

Each 15-minute show features one or two mermaids who remain underwater for the duration, using both the hookah lines and breath-hold techniques (to help the performance look more natural). The mermaids glide through the water like a real Ariel in colorful tails and fins, interacting with crowds through the glass, often to the amazement of young visitors. Janise (who states she's been in the water every day since 2009 and may actually be a mermaid herself) also runs the Mermaid School, where guests can swim and learn underwater dance moves while wearing a monofin and tail.

Address 3333 Blue Diamond Road, Las Vegas, NV 89139, +1 (702) 263-7777, www.silvertoncasino.com/hotel/aquarium-mermaid-show, info@silvertoncasino.com | Getting there Bus 217 to Dean Martin before Blue Diamond | Hours Thu–Sat noon–8pm, Sun 10:30am–6:30pm | Tip View the highly regarded Cirque du Soleil show *O*, which incorporates artistic swimming and divers (3600 Las Vegas Boulevard South, www.cirquedusoleil.com/o).

62 Mob Museum

Mafia courthouse turned organized-crime museum

With the mob playing a pivotal role in shaping Las Vegas into its glittering gambling oasis, it's fitting that a museum dedicated to its activities has found its home here. The Mob Museum focuses on organized crime, both in Las Vegas and around the country. Located inside what was once the federal courthouse, the museum is home to dozens of exhibits and hundreds of artifacts to preserve the history and stories of mob activity and the tactics by law enforcement to end it. The impressive building, designed in a neoclassical style vastly different from its surrounding buildings, was the first federal structure in Las Vegas when it was built in 1933.

The courtroom regularly held cases involving mobsters and organized crime, including the 1950 Kefauver hearings. The hearings questioned individuals like Wilbur Clark of the Desert Inn, Moe Sedway of the Flamingo, and Nevada Lieutenant Governor Clifford Jones about organized crime in the Vegas casino industry. These hearings spurred Congress to pass gambling bans across the country, solidifying Las Vegas' role as the capital of American gambling and, unintentionally, increasing mob activity in the city as gangs from all over the country headed here to continue their empires.

When all occupants of the building moved in 2005, the federal government gave the building to the city for free, under the condition that it be historically preserved and used for a cultural purpose. Then-Mayor Oscar Goodman (who at one time was a prominent defense attorney who regularly represented alleged mobsters) came up with the idea to use the building for the museum. Preservation architects worked to restore the building to its original grandeur by removing traces of modern renovations, uncovering the original paint colors, and recreating some traditional lighting fixtures in preparation for the museum's opening in 2012.

Address 300 Stewart Avenue, Las Vegas, NV 89101, +1 (702) 229-2734, www.themobmuseum.org | Getting there Deuce on the Strip Bus to EB Stewart after 4th or Downtown Loop Bus to Mob Museum | Hours Daily 9am–9pm | Tip Make your way to North First Street between Ogden and Stewart Avenues to see the Block 16 historical marker, where crime ran rampant in the '20s and '30s.

63 Mondays Dark at The Space

Biweekly variety show for charity

The Space, a 3,000-square-foot community-driven and charity-based arts complex, is one of the newest and coolest spaces to see live entertainment in Las Vegas. Featuring cabarets, live music, fashion shows, plays, and burlesque revues, The Space is a trendy and eclectic venue with state-of-the-art staging and Audio and Visual equipment, a customizable floor plan, and full bar. Owned by Mark Shunock, performer known for *Rock of Ages* and the in-arena announcer for the Golden Knights, it is an outpost of the Entertainment Community Fund.

Their flagship show is *Mondays Dark*, a biweekly variety show that raises money for a new charity each night. Started in 2013 by Shunock and Cheryl Daro, the name was inspired by how Broadway shows (and many on-Strip shows) are typically "dark" on Monday nights. Their goal is to raise $10,000 during 90 minutes of "chat, entertainment, and a lot of laughs." Each year, they give to 21 local nonprofits, keeping all money in the community. So far, they have raised over $2 million for more than 200 local nonprofits like the Miracle League of Las Vegas, Nevada SPCA, and USO Las Vegas, and have over 300 charities on their waitlist. The creators wanted to make an event unlike anything out there that perfectly exemplifies Las Vegas: over-the-top, a little crude, but unapologetically community-driven. As announcer Shunock tells the crowd, "Whether the money comes from an event like this or a gala with bad chicken, it doesn't make a difference."

Named "Best of the City" by *Vegas Seven* and "Best of Vegas" by *Las Vegas Weekly*, it's the city's first variety show for a cause. The audience can expect plenty of banter from Shunock and his co-hosts, with music (often to a central theme) and conversations with invited guests. Past performers include local musicians and bands, and standouts like Wayne Newton, Brad Garrett, and Shania Twain.

Address 3460 Cavaretta Court, Las Vegas, NV 89103, +1 (702) 903-1070, www.thespacelv.com, info@thespacelv.com | **Getting there** Bus 202 to Flamingo after Rio | **Hours** See website for scheduled events | **Tip** Check out a Golden Knights game at T-Mobile Arena to hear Shunock announcing (3787 Las Vegas Boulevard South, www.nhl.com/goldenknights).

64 Mt. Charleston CCC Sites

Explore the mountain cultivated in the 1930s

Started as part of Franklin Roosevelt's New Deal, the Civilian Conservation Corps (CCC) was a voluntary work relief program that ran from 1933 to 1942 for unemployed, unmarried men aged 18 to 25. Their goal was to conserve the country's natural resources while providing jobs for young men. They are responsible for many of our country's most well-known natural areas like Great Smoky Mountains National Park and Acadia National Park.

Here in Southern Nevada, the CCC started Camp Charleston Mountain in the Spring Mountains to the west of Las Vegas. During the summers (the workers moved to a camp closer to the city for winters to avoid the heavy snowfall and dangerous conditions), the Civilian Conservation Corps built trails, a ranger station, water system, and several campgrounds that either still remain, or enabled the park to further develop to what it is today. The most notable locations that remain are the Cathedral Rock picnic area and the Foxtail snow play area. The Acastus Trail features historic buildings that were once used by the CCC, and the Mahogany Grove Trail features camp stoves left from one of the first campgrounds set up by the CCC and educational panels that tell the story of the men responsible for much of the infrastructure found on the mountain.

Roosevelt actually visited Camp Charleston Mountain when he came to Southern Nevada in 1935 for the dedication of the Hoover Dam. He took the short trip to see how the CCC was getting along. But up on the mountain, the president's driver got lost and when he tried to turn around on a narrow road, they barely avoided tumbling down the side of a steep slope.

Today, the Spring Mountains are an important and immensely popular recreation resource that provides relief from the heat in the summer (temperatures can be as much as 30 degrees cooler in the mountains) and the ability to play in snow in the winter.

Address Deer Creek Road, Mount Charleston, NV 89124, +1 (702) 872-5486, www.gomtcharleston.com/mahogany-grove | Getting there By car, take 95N to exit 96 to NV-157/Kyle Canyon Road | Hours Open 24 hours unless closed for seasonal or emergency conditions | Tip Head to nearby Lee Canyon for hiking in the summer and skiing in the winter (6725 Lee Canyon Road, www.leecanyonlv.com).

65__Nellis Dunes

View the entire valley from here

Just north of Nellis Air Force Base, between Las Vegas Boulevard and I-15, is an expanse of desert called the Nellis Dunes Off-Highway Vehicle (OHV) Recreation Area. The area is home to large sand dunes with an array of trails for adrenaline junkies and off-road enthusiasts. But what's surprising is the amazing view of the entire Valley that this desolate location offers.

The Nellis Dunes were officially designated as an off-highway area in 2014 and are owned by the Bureau of Land Management, like much of the surrounding nature in Clark County. The area is over 10,035 acres, with 900 allocated to Clark County for the OHV park. Tour groups offer excursions to the dunes to experience the trails that range from beginner to expert on vehicles like sandrails, motorcycles, and ATVs.

Even if you're not up for any off-road action, heading out to the dunes is a great way to experience Nevada's desert landscape without even leaving the city. While any time of day is amazing to visit, one magical time is after sunset. Viewing the valley from the dunes, you can see the glowing lights of the city, both the amber-hued homes and the neon lights of the Strip, completely encircled by a wall of darkness. It puts in perspective just how remote Las Vegas is compared to other metropolitan areas, while showing off its impressive and vibrant entertainment district.

Due to its proximity to Nellis Air Force Base and its location in the direct flight path of departing aircraft, the dunes were never developed. Now that the BLM protects the land, it will remain public and avoid being developed into homes or warehouse spaces. The dunes are the perfect escape from the bustle of the city without venturing too far afield. Try out an off-road experience on the dunes, view the glittering city lights across the valley, or catch a glimpse of the stars with a little clearer skies and slightly less light pollution.

Address Las Vegas Boulevard North, Las Vegas, NV 89115, +1 (702) 515-5000, www.blm.gov/visit/nellis-dunes | Getting there By car, take I-15 N to exit 58 to NV-604 toward Apex/Nellis AFB, take Las Vegas Boulevard South to the parking lot | Hours Unrestricted for parking lot access; dawn–dusk for off-roading | Tip Aviation enthusiasts can use the Nellis Dunes as a vantage point to watch military aircraft take off and land during regular training exercises.

66 Nelson's Ghost Town

Abandoned land of lawlessness, greed, and murder

The town of Nelson (population 37) was once called El Dorado, or "guilded one," by Spanish explorers who discovered gold in the area in 1775. In the mid 1800s, miners and prospectors flocked west trying to strike it rich during the Gold Rush (some to avoid the Civil War draft). The area was inundated with prospectors who wanted to mine the nearby Techatticup Mine (named after the Paiute word for "hungry"), which immediately caused disputes with those who were already established there.

Nelson was the epitome of an Old West town with shootouts and murders part of daily life. One story claims that during the peak of criminal activity, local law enforcement wouldn't even enter the area.

The Techatticup Mine remained active until the mid 1940s, with another boost from illegal moonshine operations during Prohibition. The mine produced millions of dollars in gold, silver, copper, and lead, and became the largest and most productive mine in the entire Colorado Mining District, before succumbing to the decline in the mining industry.

After it had sat abandoned for decades, Tony and Bobbie Werly bought the Techatticup land in 1993. They purchased 14 former mine buildings that had been moved off property (for $1 from the Bureau of Land Management) and began restoring them. The Werlys now live at the mine and have turned their interest in collecting and restoration into a free open-air museum. Visitors can also take paid guided tours to one of the oldest mines in Southern Nevada to explore some of the tunnels and the relics left behind. Shootings still happen here daily, though this time it's photography shoots. From the antique rusted cars to the abandoned Chevron station, movie props left from sets (like the plane from *3000 Miles to Graceland*), and the mine itself, it has become a favorite for local photographers to capture a variety of interesting backdrops.

Address 16880 State Highway 165, Nelson, NV 89046, +1 (702) 291-0026, www.eldoradocanyonminetours.com, goldmine1861@gmail.com | Getting there By car, take I-95 South towards Searchlight, turn left onto NV-165 | Hours Daily 8am–4pm, call ahead for tour reservations | Tip For another abandoned site, check out Southern Nevada's oldest mining area at Potosi (Pahrump Valley Highway at Mount Potosi Canyon Road, Spring Mountains, www.shpo.nv.gov/nevadas-historical-markers/historical-markers/potosi).

67_Neon Museum Las Vegas

Disused neon brought back to life

"The city of Las Vegas, as far as I am concerned, owes the signs… a lot of the credit for building the city because it creates an atmosphere of excitement and fun… They just have fun here," said Betty Willis, the renowned designer known for the "Welcome to Las Vegas" sign.

The Neon Museum, a mesmerizing outdoor gallery of colossal artwork, preserves and displays iconic neon signs. Started as a non-profit in 1996, it celebrates the artistry and cultural significance of these signs while showcasing their stories and the evolution of Vegas itself. The museum's collection contains over 800 signs from over 200 properties, some dating back to the 1930s.

The boneyard, a name used for where out-of-use items are stored, is a controlled chaos of more than 250 signs that light up the night sky, including renowned pieces like the Stardust, Riviera, and Flamingo signs, plus the Hard Rock guitar. The vibrant pink Moulin Rouge script greets visitors entering the boneyard. The Moulin Rouge Hotel opened in 1955 as the first racially integrated hotel and casino in Las Vegas. During its short run, it was a landmark for the civil rights movement, attracting entertainers like Sammy Davis Jr., Nat King Cole, and Louis Armstrong. The sign was designed by Willis and is done in her handwriting, inspired by French-style lettering, to pay homage to the hotel's namesake in Paris.

Currently, 28 signs have been returned to their former glory, with the museum typically restoring one to two each year and regularly rearranging the boneyard to highlight different signs as their collection grows. "Brilliant!" created by artist Craig Winslow is an immersive audiovisual experience in the North Gallery that uses projection mapping to bring signs to life that have not yet been restored or are beyond repair. The show is a glimpse into the past, highlighting just how ingrained the signs are in city history.

Address 770 Las Vegas Boulevard North, Las Vegas, NV 89101, +1 (702) 387-6366, www.neonmuseum.org | Getting there Deuce on the Strip Bus to Stewart after 4th or Bus 113 to Las Vegas before Cashman | Hours Check the website for opening hours | Tip Visit the landmark "Welcome to Fabulous Las Vegas" sign, the most famous neon sign in the world (5100 Las Vegas Boulevard South).

68 Nevada Veterans Memorial

Sculptures commemorating sacrifice and valor

Found on two acres just outside the Grant Sawyer State Office Building, the Nevada State Veterans Memorial is a tribute to service members from both Nevada and across the country. American Shooters, Inc., a local veteran-operated business, initiated the project in 2009 as a national tribute funded privately by contributions from businesses and individuals around the US. The memorial provides a quiet and introspective place to contemplate the common bond of service and express a debt of gratitude to all generations of American veterans and their families for their sacrifice and dedication.

The memorial consists of ten 7.5-foot-tall aluminum sculptures. They are arranged in a line in front of massive asymmetrical black granite walls bearing etched quotes describing the veteran experience. The statues depict service members from each major American conflict, ranging from the Revolutionary War, including an American soldier and a Native American warrior, up to the Gulf War with a fighter pilot. Aluminum, artist Douwe Blumberg explains, was chosen for the historic statues to give them a "ghostlike" quality as if peering through time. But, looking closely, the statues appear to be squinting, as if they are really standing among visitors in the bright desert sun.

In the center of the memorial is a bronze vignette representing the Global War on Terror with contemporary figures from multiple military branches. A final sculpture in bronze shows four figures – a veteran, his wife, and two children – and is dedicated to military families for their support and sacrifice.

At the memorial's dedication in 2016, Blumberg said he wanted the project to be large, in scope, scale, and vision. "It's a timeline of service, a continuum, formed by generation after generation of veterans. That timelessness and the commonality. Something that would communicate more scope than a specific battle, incident, or conflict."

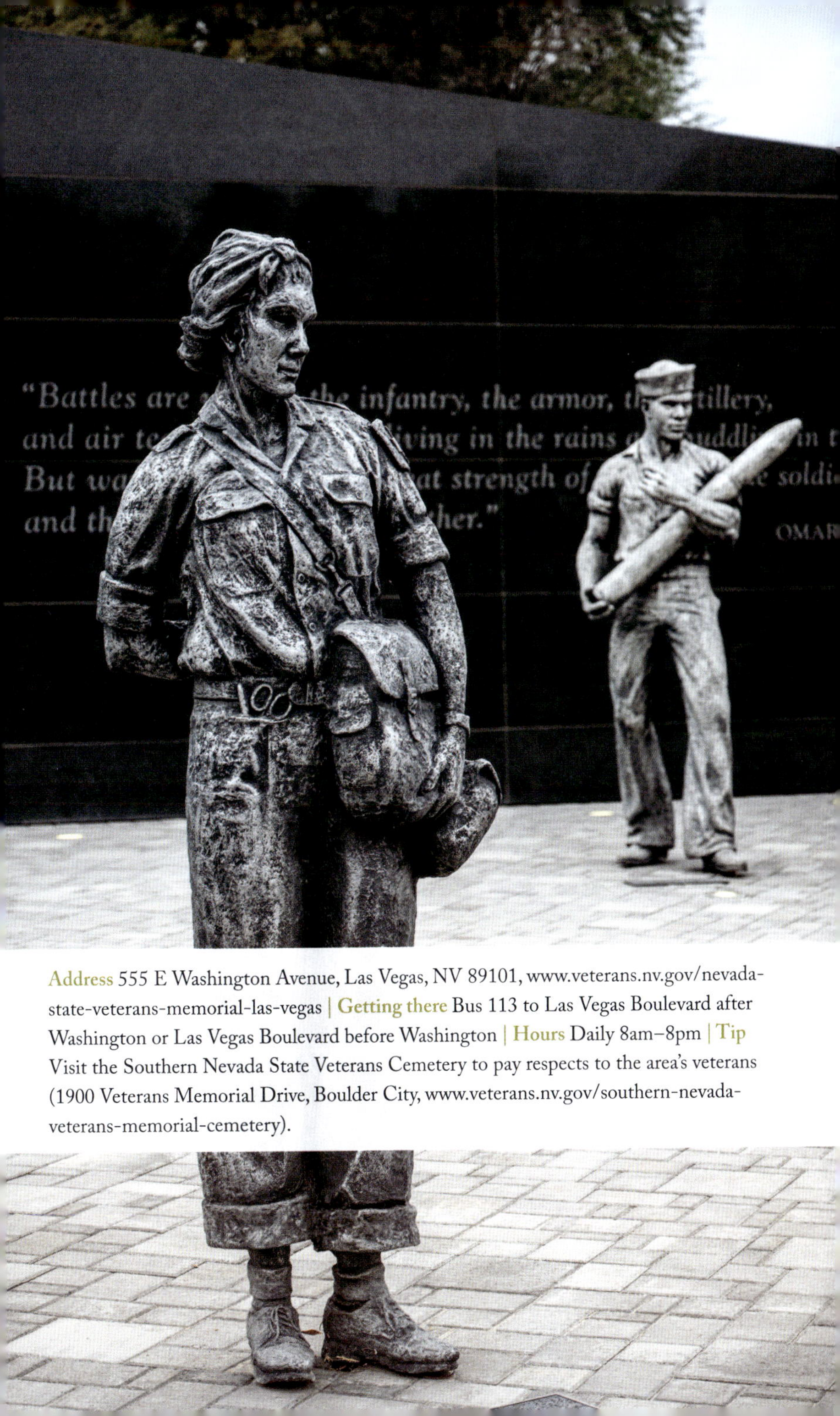

Address 555 E Washington Avenue, Las Vegas, NV 89101, www.veterans.nv.gov/nevada-state-veterans-memorial-las-vegas | **Getting there** Bus 113 to Las Vegas Boulevard after Washington or Las Vegas Boulevard before Washington | **Hours** Daily 8am–8pm | **Tip** Visit the Southern Nevada State Veterans Cemetery to pay respects to the area's veterans (1900 Veterans Memorial Drive, Boulder City, www.veterans.nv.gov/southern-nevada-veterans-memorial-cemetery).

69 Nuwu Art Gallery

POC-owned creative hub and gallery

In a city exploding with creative expression, Nuwu Art + Activism Studios is a fundamental piece of the local scene, fusing art, activism, and Indigenous culture. Nuwu Studios is a creative hub founded by Southern Paiute artist and activist Fawn Douglas. The term "Nuwu" translates to "the people" in the Southern Paiute language, reflecting the studios' commitment to community and cultural empowerment.

Established in 2020, the studios have become a cornerstone for Black, Indigenous, and People of Color (BIPOC) artists. The space fosters collaboration among artists and activities, hosting workshops, exhibitions, and educational events that promote cultural revitalization and decolonization.

Douglas, a graduate of the UNLV Master of Fine Arts program, is an accomplished artist, working in mediums of painting, weaving, sculpture, and performance, all deeply informed by her heritage. "My art draws me closer to my Nuwu culture and identity," she says. "Many pieces operate as a filter that keeps the integrity of sacred information that my people hold dear, while allowing Nuwuvi culture to be shared with a broader audience."

The gallery and community center on Maryland Parkway serve as the public-facing arm of the studios. They hosts exhibitions from local artists on a rotating basis, showcasing the work of people of color (POC) and exploring themes of cultural heritage and community building. Admission to the gallery is free and open to the public. Donations may be made to the IndigenousAF nonprofit, which helps to continue the work of the studios and provides more opportunities for local artists like those in the Nuwu Art Collective: a group of diverse artists, sharing studio space and engaging in various creative practices, drawing from Native American, Indigenous Latin American, and African American traditions to strengthen cultural knowledge and identity through art.

Address 1331 S Maryland Parkway, Las Vegas, NV 89104, +1 (775) 751-7800, www.nuwuart.com | Getting there Bus 109 to Maryland before Franklin or Maryland after Franklin | Hours Thu & Fri 5–8pm, Sat noon–4pm | Tip Visit the Marjorie Barrick Museum of Art at UNLV to view pieces from the College of Fine Arts (4505 S Maryland Parkway, www.unlv.edu/barrickmuseum).

70_Oddfellows

A nightclub for people who don't like nightclubs

The gaming culture in Vegas goes hand in hand with its nightlife scene. From the early days of Paul Anka's Jubilation to today's Drai's and Hakkasan, the city's nightclubs remain overwhelmingly popular. But many, both locals and tourists alike, have no interest in these types of venues with their strict dress codes, high prices, and incessant thrum of mainstream electronic club anthems. One place taking a different approach to clubs is the downtown Oddfellows.

Oddfellows bills itself as an inclusive, judgment-free alternative to the Vegas nightlife scene. Opened in 2015 with a complete renovation in 2024, it's "an institution for the offbeat," according to *Las Vegas Weekly*. With a decor comprising dark antique photos, drawn skulls, retro TVs playing music videos, pinball machines, and gothic chandeliers, it's a drastic departure from a typical club in Vegas. Its front bar is a relatively quiet and intimate area where you can escape to talk or take a breather on the couch before heading to the dance floor. As for the dance floor, there are two. One large open area with high ceilings and a disco ball, and a second, smaller one in the back lounge with more couches and another bar.

For music, there seems to be something for all tastes. With themed nights like Nu Metal, Emo, K-pop, '80s, and Club Classics, the club transforms into a venue for everyone. And that might be what sets Oddfellows apart. It's not just its quirky decor or alternative vibe, but that it is interested in giving the people what they need in a nightclub. Oddfellows' director of marketing and events told *Las Vegas Weekly*, "We were just synthesizing feedback and talking to folks in the community, younger folks, DJs, and the regulars to see if there are any gaps." As the publication aptly put it: "In a city where authenticity within the nightlife scene is a rare commodity, Oddfellows stands out."

Address 150 Las Vegas Boulevard N #190, Las Vegas, NV 89101, www.oddfellowslv.com, info@oddfellowslv.com | **Getting there** Deuce on the Strip Bus to Las Vegas Boulevard at Fremont Street Experience | **Hours** Tue–Sun 8pm–3am | **Tip** To experience a nightclub that is very much a nightclub, try Omnia at Caesars Palace (3570 Las Vegas Boulevard South, www.caesars.com/caesars-palace/things-to-do/nightlife/omnia-nightclub).

71 Old Country Boots

Custom boots for cowboys or wannabes

A city born from ranchers, the Old West and cowboy culture never truly left Vegas. Many of the city's early casinos, like the El Rancho and Last Frontier, were themed after the Old West to play into visitors' preconceived ideas of the isolated frontier settlement. The love for cowboy culture remains today, with many heading to Vegas for the Old West experience. One place that caters to this crowd is Old Country Boots. Located just east of the airport, this family-run small business was founded by Javier Martell. Javier grew up around horses and was no stranger to cowboy boots.

After he had the opportunity to take a boot-making class, he fell in love with the craft and almost immediately started his business. He spent five years growing Old Country Boots in his garage before opening the storefront, which is filled with the intoxicating rich and earthy scent of leather. His hand-crafted boots can be made from more than 25 types of animal skins, including exotic pelts like elephant, giraffe, alligator, and ostrich, which are purchased from animal sanctuaries whose animals have died of natural causes.

Javier designs all of the boots by hand and they are 100 percent leather. While he does create some ready-to-wear styles, the majority of his sales are from custom boots. After making an appointment, customers have their feet measured by hand to make the perfect foot mold, or "last", that will be used to create their boots. Then, working with Javier, you'll choose the leather, create a design, and select a shape (for example, round or square toes), and then Javier and his team get to work, taking anywhere from 60 to 400 working hours depending on the design.

His boots are now so in demand, they have a waiting list of nearly six months for custom orders. The shop is particularly popular during "Cowboy Christmas," held during the Wrangler National Finals Rodeo held in Las Vegas each December.

Address 2450 Chandler Avenue, Las Vegas, NV 89120, +1 (702) 664-9198, www.oldcountryboots.com, javier@oldcountryboots.com | Getting there Bus 212 to Sunset after Eastern | Hours Mon noon–6pm, Tue–Fri 10am–6pm, Sat & Sun by appointment | Tip For a laid-back "industrial country-chic" bar, head to Horse Trailer Hideout (1506 S Main Street, www.horsetrailerhideout.com).

72 One of Vegas' Oldest Houses

Houses built for the railroad still stand downtown

Las Vegas was built by the railroad. Between 1909 and 1911, the San Pedro, Los Angeles, and Salt Lake Railroad constructed "railroad cottages" near Second, Third, and Fourth streets downtown to house the workers flocking to the new desert town. "The development was the first subdivision in Las Vegas," historian Mark Hall-Patton told the *Las Vegas Review-Journal*. "And one of the first in the country where all the homes were identical." The small two-to-three-bedroom homes were constructed with concrete cinder blocks that were inexpensive and helped keep the homes warmer in the winter and cooler in the summer. However, this didn't completely protect its inhabitants. George Garner, born in 1923, grew up in two of the cottages. In a 2005 *Review-Journal* article, he recalled sleeping on the porch in the summer.

A total of 64 homes were built to revive the failing "Clark's Las Vegas Townsite" and bring in upper-level employees, like conductors, engineers, brakemen, and even a railroad surgeon. The rent at the time was \$18–\$20 per month, about four times higher than that of wooden homes. After the boom of the railroad, the need to house workers dwindled. Many houses were knocked down to make room for the commercialization of the area. Thankfully, some were transplanted: three to the Springs Preserve and one to the Clark County Museum in Henderson. Only an estimated four remain in their original locations, though Hall-Patton said he was only able to verify two.

The remaining houses, one at 608 3rd Street and one at 629 Casino Center, are now occupied by businesses, one a law firm and one a bail bondsman. While neither inhabitant originally knew of their homes' legacies, they both liked that they were connected to a small piece of history. "I brag about it all the time," bail bondsman Andy Renshaw told the *Review-Journal*.

Address 608 S 3rd Street, Las Vegas, NV 89101 | **Getting there** Deuce on the Strip Bus or Bus 113 to Bonneville Transit Center | **Hours** Viewable from the outside only | **Tip** To see another remnant of the railroad, head to Bonanza Underpass, built in 1937 to allow safe passage from downtown to the western part of the city (W Bonanza Road near N Main Street).

73_Original McCarran Entrance

Preserved entrance to Las Vegas' first airport

Harry Reid International Airport is one of the busiest in the country, with thousands of people traveling through each day. First opened as Alamo Field in 1943 by aviator George Crockett (descendant of frontiersman Davy Crockett) and renamed McCarran Field in 1948, it quickly became the most popular way for people to visit Las Vegas from far afield. During this time, the entrance to the airport was on Route 91, now known as Las Vegas Boulevard, and consisted of one small adobe-style terminal not far from the road. The stone gateway that marked the original entrance to the airport can still be seen today at the Executive Terminal just south of the "Welcome to Las Vegas" sign.

The gateway consists of two 25-ton stone pillars affixed with a sign between them stating "McCarran Field." These pillars were constructed from native Southern Nevada rock in 1941 and placed outside of the original McCarran Field, which is now Nellis Air Force Base in the northeast. When Alamo Field was renamed (and the air base was changed to Las Vegas AFB), the pillars were moved to their current location. The *Review-Journal* reported on December 6, 1948, "Each will be transported separately to the new field which will be dedicated as 'McCarran Field' on Dec. 19." On opening day, an air show with military aircraft was held.

During this time the airport had 12 daily flights served by Western Air Express, Transcontinental Western Airlines, Bonanza, and United. This entrance on Route 91 remained in place until 1963 when the entrance was moved to its current location on Paradise Road to facilitate the more than one million annual passengers heading in and out of the booming city. The original terminal building remained on site until 1995, when it was demolished to make room for the executive terminal buildings.

Address 6005 Las Vegas Boulevard South, Las Vegas, NV 89119, +1 (702) 261-5211, www.harryreidairport.com | Getting there Deuce on the Strip Bus to Las Vegas Sign | Hours Unrestricted | Tip Stop into Harry Reid to see the Cannon Aviation Museum and learn about the history of commercial and general aviation in Southern Nevada (25 Wayne Newton Boulevard, www.harryreidairport.com/museum).

74_Pedal and Pour

Bike and coffee shop creating community in LV

Las Vegas' coffee scene has been seeing a revitalization in the last few years with local roasters and specialty shops popping up all over the valley. Pedal and Pour, in the Southwest, is a seemingly peculiar combination coffee and bike shop that has become a hub for the valley's cycling community. Opened in 2021 by Dan Kalny and Dave Calica, they aimed to create a feeling of community in a city not known for its cycling. The shop was inspired by a bike shop and a nearby café in Indiana, where Kalny went to school. He and his riding group would grab coffee after a ride or while waiting for their bike repairs. Aiming to replicate that feeling, they opened Pedal and Pour to combine the cyclists' needs with gear and repairs while offering a community space with great coffee and snacks.

But what was important to Kalny and Calica was that the coffee shop didn't feel like an afterthought but one that featured high-quality products. Drinks are brewed with the locally roasted Vesta beans that are brought in fresh each week, and feature in a large menu of regular items and specialty seasonal drinks. Their pastries are delivered daily, made by a two-Michelin-star chef. The word has spread, making it a hub both for cyclists stopping in to get new bike accessories or a quick bike repair, and for locals to grab a drink on their way to work or on their dog walk.

Outside the shop, they offer regular weekly rides – with their most popular being the Sunday morning "recovery ride," great for faster riders to recover from a heavy night or for those new to cycling to have a slower and less stressful experience. Kalny says it's very important to create a community welcoming to all skill levels, whether you have top-of-the-line equipment or a bike you found on Marketplace. Pedal and Pour takes the intimidation out of cycling, making the shop a place for anyone in, and out, of the cycling community to grab a great drink.

Address 9742 W Maule Avenue, Las Vegas, NV 89148, +1 (725) 992-3462, www.pedalpour.com, pedalandpourcafe@gmail.com | **Getting there** Bus 120 to Fort Apache after Maule | **Hours** Mon 7am–4pm, Tue–Fri 7am–6pm, Sat 7am–4pm, Sun 7am–3pm | **Tip** For highly rated and locally roasted coffee, check out Yaw Farm Coffee Roasters (7034 W Charleston Boulevard, www.instagram.com/yawfarmcoffee).

75 Pinball Hall of Fame

Retro paradise on the Strip

On Las Vegas Boulevard South, near the "Welcome to Las Vegas" sign, is the Pinball Hall of Fame. Housed in a boxy warehouse covered in larger-than-life letters, it is a hands-on museum with playable pinball machines and vintage arcade games. Stepping inside is like walking into a fever dream of electronic bells and whistles – the casino floor times ten.

As a project of the Las Vegas Pinball Collectors Club, the museum features nearly 700 machines from many eras, including very rare ones like Williams' Black Gold and Bally's Pinball Circus, as well as some classic video arcade games and novelty machines.

Run by long-time arcade owner Tim Arnold, it is fully staffed by volunteers and is completely funded by donations. It was first opened in 2006 and bounced around to a few locations until, in summer 2021, it found its current home in the 28,000-square-foot warehouse specifically built to house the Hall of Fame.

While pinball came about sometime before the 1930s, the game could have started around WWII, the 1870s, or possibly back in the 1500s with table versions, depending on who you ask. Machines as we know them today started in the 1970s with solid-state electronics and digital displays. Pinball boomed in the 1980s as games started incorporating full soundtracks, elaborate light shows, and animations into their machines. Movie and character licenses cropped up with *Indiana Jones*, *Star Trek*, and *The Addams Family* being extremely popular. Though pinball and arcades took a downturn in the 1990s with the advent of the home computer, collectors and game enthusiasts like Tim Arnold have made it a purpose to collect and restore the machines. Long-time pinball enthusiasts heading to the Hall of Fame can find classics like Elton John's *Captain Fantastic*, while new gamers can find more contemporary machines like *Guardians of the Galaxy*, while exploring the endless rows of these classic games.

Address 4925 Las Vegas Boulevard South, Las Vegas, NV 89119, +1 (702) 597-2627, www.pinballmuseum.org, pinballhalloffame@msn.com | Getting there Bus 212 to Sunset after Sandhill | Hours Sun–Thu 10am–9pm, Fri & Sat 10am–10pm | Tip For a more modern game, check out *Zero Latency*, a multiplayer virtual-reality gaming experience (3799 Las Vegas Boulevard South, www.zerolatencyvr.com/en/locations/las-vegas).

76 Pioneer Saloon

Visit the oldest bar in Southern Nevada

About 25 miles south of Las Vegas is the remote desert town of Goodsprings. Once a thriving mining town, it has since dwindled to fewer than 200 people, making it, technically, a living ghost town. It was named for Joseph Good, a cattle rancher whose livestock frequented a spring found near the town. In 1856, Mormon miners found lead in the Potosi Mountain, and gold was found in 1893. It was once the most productive mining district in Clark County with lead, silver, copper, zinc, and gold all in the vicinity. The town's largest boom happened around 1910 thanks to the railroad's interest.

Pioneer Saloon, the town's most famous site, was established in 1913 by Clark County Commissioner George Fayle and is considered the oldest saloon in Clark County, and one of the oldest saloons in all of Nevada. The saloon and Fayle's other establishment, Hotel Fayle, were the cultural hub of the town.

The saloon's 100-plus-year history is full of intrigue, movie stars, and possible hauntings. On June 27, 1915, Joe Armstrong shot Paul Coski twice over a dispute during a card game, killing him on the spot (bullet holes can still be seen in the pressed tin walls). He was found not guilty because it was ruled self-defense. In 1942, Hollywood star Clark Gable waited at the bar, drunk and "inconsolable" as rescuers attempted to find his wife Carole Lombard's body after her plane crashed at nearby Mount Potosi. The bar has also featured in movies like *The Mexican*, *Miss Congeniality*, and a deleted scene from *Fear and Loathing in Las Vegas*. It also features as "Prospector Saloon" in the video game *Fallout: New Vegas*.

A mix of a biker bar and old-school western saloon, the bar is still a thriving venue in the otherwise desolate Mojave. You can elbow up to the bar next to locals and tourists from every corner of the world to feel a bit of history before heading further out into the desert.

Address 310 West Spring Street, Goodsprings, NV 89019, +1 (702) 674-6809, www.pioneersaloonnv.com | Getting there By car, take I-15 S to exit 12, then NV-161 W to Goodsprings | Hours Sun–Thu 9am–10pm, Fri & Sat 9am–midnight | Tip Stop at the Goodsprings Cemetery just as you enter town to discover graves dating back to 1890 and see what inspired portions of the game *Fallout: New Vegas* (101 W Springs Street, Jean).

77_Pole Fitness Studio

Fitness classes fit for Las Vegas

Fawnia Mondey, owner of Pole Fitness Studio in Spring Valley, is considered the world's first pole fitness instructor. When she began her career as an exotic dancer in the '90s, pole dancing was beginning to add more athletic movements like climbing, spinning, and inversions to the burlesque-style striptease popular in the '60s. When Fawnia tried to find a pole dancing school to learn moves, she discovered, "There's no such thing, you just get up there and dance." After she mastered the Fireman (a spinning move that mimics sliding down a firepole), she made flyers and promoted her teaching services. By the end of 1994, Fawnia was teaching exotic dancing lessons to other dancers in the club before opening.

Fawnia went on to open the Exotic Dance School and produce the instructional video *Pole Work, Volume 1*, which launched her career as an instructor to a larger audience. When she moved to Las Vegas in 2005, she shifted her focus to a more fitness-forward approach. This made her business grow from having primarily strippers in her classes to also teachers, nurses, and law-enforcement officers who were looking for a fun way to get in shape.

Fawnia's pole dancing classes provide a full-body and mind workout to improve cardio fitness and increase strength and flexibility. Her classes offer a fun and supportive environment where students celebrate each other's successes. Fawnia says, "Even if you're hesitant, start today. You'll never be this young again." There are classes for all skill levels with many focusing on beginner-friendly walks, spins, and transitions paired with exciting choreography set to your favorite dance tracks. Students say Fawnia's warm and inclusive classes have not only improved their fitness but have also boosted their self-confidence. For those who want something beyond fitness, they also offer classes on burlesque, lap dance, and twerk, as well as group classes for bachelorette and other parties.

Address 4265 S Arville Street, Suite A, Las Vegas, NV 89103, +1 (702) 878-7653, www.polefitnessstudio.com, support@polefitnessstudio.com | Getting there Bus 202 to Flamingo before Arville or Flamingo after Arville | Hours See website for class schedule | Tip For a different form of exercise class, try Las Vegas Boxing (5465 Simmons Street, Suite 8, www.lasvegasboxingclub.com).

78 The Punk Rock Museum

Play your favorite punk rocker's guitar

Opened in April 2023, The Punk Rock Museum is quickly becoming a favorite museum in Las Vegas. Co-founder, NOFX frontman Mike "Fat Mike" Burkett, originally came to Las Vegas to start a punk shop with some memorabilia, but it morphed into what is now a 12,000-square-foot museum that houses artifacts from punk's origins in the 1960s up until today. With a tattoo parlor and full bar, The Punk Rock Museum is not your average exhibition. The founders, including Burkett, Vinnie Fiorello, and Mona Whetzel, to name a few, wanted the museum to be polished and respectable but still have the same grit and visceral feeling of punk. They wanted it to be a testament to the culture, calling it a living museum, constantly changing and updating, the same way punk has evolved and changed over time.

One of the most popular exhibits includes the 1966 Telecaster Joe Strummer used during his time with The Clash. The guitar had originally been on display at the Rock & Roll Hall of Fame, when his wife and children decided Strummer would rather it be among punk rock's finest.

On the museum's second floor is the Jam Room, home to dozens of guitars from both popular and lesser-known artists. This one-of-a-kind interactive room encourages visitors to pick up and play the instruments to recreate their favorite guitarist's sound by using their exact guitar and amp setup. Knowledgeable attendants help you get set up and even teach you a few chords or maybe a bridge to a popular punk song. Rob Ruckus, caretaker of the Jam Room, says, "You're not going to hurt them," displaying the severely scratched back side of Rancid's Tim Armstrong's guitar.

Whether you love punk, have never listened to a note, or aren't even sure what it is, the museum is still for you. When asked if you needed to be "punk" to visit the museum, co-founder Mona Whetzel said, "Do you have to be a dinosaur to visit a history museum?"

Address 1422 Western Avenue, Las Vegas, NV 89102, +1 (702) 823-2983, www.thepunkrockmuseum.com, info@thepunkrockmuseum.com | Getting there CX Centennial Express Bus to Grand Central at Las Vegas Premium Outlets | Hours Mon–Fri noon–8pm, Sat & Sun 10am–8pm | Tip Visit Double Down Saloon for free punk shows (4640 Paradise Road, www.doubledownsaloon.com).

79 Radial Symmetry

Giant sculpture honoring Paiute craftsmanship

Downtown, two towering stainless steel circular structures rise from the pavement on the median where Main meets Commerce. Each stands 16 by 16 feet and weighs 10 tons. Together they form *Radial Symmetry*, a sculpture designed to enhance the visual landscape of the Arts District and, as the artist Luis Varela-Rico says, serve as "a gateway for the future of the City of Las Vegas."

Radial Symmetry was installed in 2018 as part of the City of Las Vegas Public Art Collection, which displays a diverse range of artworks, from murals to large-scale sculptures, celebrating the city's culture, history, and creative spirit and the Main Street Improvement Project to revitalize downtown Las Vegas.

The abstract cylindrical forms of *Radial Symmetry*, which almost resemble fan blades or turbines, were inspired by traditional Southern Paiute basket weaving. "For generations, the nomadic tribes took great pride in developing intricate and beautiful ways to create and adorn their baskets," Valeria-Rico explains. The sculpture honors the care and craftsmanship Paiute people used to "individualize and beautify an ordinary utilitarian object." The sculpture translates the use of willow or sumac fibers used for basketmaking into steel, through curves and patterns that suggest motion and symmetry, form and function, past and present.

Born in Guadalajara, Mexico and raised in Las Vegas, Varela-Rico is known for his large-scale public works that fuse art, technology, and heritage. Many of his sculptures can be found around Vegas including his *Organic Study No.2,* a 15-foot LED and steel sculpture depicting a hand holding a baseball at Desert Diamonds Baseball Complex and Norte y Sur, two steel heads in a "stare down" on the median of Eastern Avenue. His work has been recognized across state and beyond, including by former First Lady of Nevada, Katherine Sisolak: "Luis has a portfolio of work which makes Nevadans proud."

Address Intersection of S Main Street and S Commerce Street, Las Vegas, NV 89101 | Getting there Centennial Express Bus to Bonneville after 1st or Bus 215 to Bonneville Transit Center | Hours Unrestricted | Tip Venture down to Boulder City to see the sculpture of Alabam, the man with the smelliest job at the Hoover Dam (600 Nevada Way, Boulder City).

80 Rat Pack Footprints

Walk in the footsteps of legendary entertainers

The Rat Pack was an illustrious group of entertainers known for their charismatic performances and effortless camaraderie. Led by Frank Sinatra, the ensemble included icons Dean Martin, Sammy Davis Jr., Peter Lawford, and Joey Bishop. The members of the group all had separate careers in Las Vegas, performing at places like the Desert Inn, Frontier, and Flamingo, but their performances together, which started in January 1960 and took place at the Copa Room at the Sands Hotel, were what many describe as the "Golden Age of Vegas." Massive crowds were attracted to their joint performances, which included iconic songs, comedy, and banter. That same year, the group starred together in the original *Ocean's Eleven* film, which was filmed at the Sands.

During this era, whenever one member had a performance, the other members regularly made a surprise appearance. Marquees along the Strip started to feature headlines like "Dean Martin, maybe Frank, maybe Sammy."

While the group was set on entertaining crowds (Sammy Davis Jr. recalled Sinatra saying, "The idea is to hang out together, find fun with the broads, and have a great time"), the Rat Pack also made stands against segregation laws in Las Vegas. Davis, in his memoir, remembers how Sinatra, in 1953, refused to perform at the Sands unless they gave Davis a room (it was common for white-only hotels to allow popular Black performers but not allow them to stay or eat on the premises).

Today, the Venetian, which is on the site of the former Sands, still pays homage to the group and their contribution to Las Vegas history. Just out front of the casino is a plaque showing a photo of the Rat Pack in 1960 accompanied by a brass plate inlaid with the group's footprints. The footprints correspond to the approximate location where the men stood for the iconic photo in front of the Sands.

Address 3377 Las Vegas Boulevard South, Las Vegas, NV 89109 | Getting there Deuce on the Strip Bus to Las Vegas at Venetian or Las Vegas at Treasure Island | Hours Unrestricted | Tip Try Sinatra Italian Restaurant to see memorabilia and try dishes inspired by Ol' Blue Eyes (313 Las Vegas Boulevard South, www.wynnlasvegas.com/dining/fine-dining/sinatra).

81_ReBAR

Where everything is for sale, even your seat

The Arts District, what *The New York Times* calls "The Least Vegas Neighborhood in Vegas," is home to ReBAR, which can best be described as a bar in an antique store. Or is it an antique store in a bar? Either way, everything inside is for sale: the beer in the coolers, the liquor in the well, the art on the walls, and even the stools you're sitting on. ReBAR is the brainchild of entrepreneur and Emmy Award-winning TV producer Derek Stonebarger. A longtime local of Vegas, he has been a significant figure in the resurgence of the Arts District and an advocate for bettering Las Vegas as a whole.

After Stonebarger was diagnosed with cancer in 2015, he decided to dive head first into his wacky business idea, saying, "Now is the time. I'm not going to wait any more." In the middle of his chemotherapy treatment, Stonebarger signed the lease and began working on ReBAR, looking to mix his hobby with an entertainment venue. "I used to buy and sell cars," he told the *Las Vegas Review-Journal*. "Before there was Craigslist, I used the classifieds. I've always used it as a hobby and for supplemental income."

The interior is an eclectic thrift store, with almost every inch of free space covered with quirky decor like wedding photos in antique frames, neon signs, mugs strung on wire, and cuckoo clocks. The mismatched tables, chairs, and barstools give a laid-back and almost-grunge feel to the bar. That, and the cheap drinks and live music, all make it a local hotspot, even in an area with countless extraordinary and distinctive nightspots.

Aside from the novel concept and local appeal, ReBAR is dedicated to giving back to the local community. Its collection of charitable cocktails benefits local foundations like the Las Vegas Arts District, Opportunity Village, Nevada Preservation Foundation, The Huntridge Foundation, and After-School All-Stars.

Address 1225 S Main Street, Las Vegas, NV 89104, +1 (702) 998-8777, www.rebarlv.com, rebarshani@gmail.com | Getting there Deuce on the Strip Bus to 3rd after Imperial or 3rd before Imperial | Hours Mon–Thu noon–midnight, Fri & Sat noon–2am | Tip Check out the local favorite Liquid Diet for craft cocktails in an industrial, "kind of witchy" bar (1415 S Commerce Street, www.instagram.com/liquid.diet.dtlv).

82 Saginaw's Shrimp Cocktail

Try the recipe that made this dish world-famous

The creation of the shrimp cocktail is up for debate. Some say the dish originated in Mexico, some say California, and some even say the UK. But the most widely confirmed version is that this simple appetizer got its start in San Francisco. From the early 1990s, oyster cocktails were popular but depleted oyster beds and advances in refrigeration (shrimp goes bad much more quickly than oysters), saw the rise in substituting shrimp.

The shrimp cocktail made its way to land-locked Las Vegas in 1959 when Italo Ghelfi, San Francisco native and Managing Partner of the Golden Gate Casino, introduced the 50-cent appetizer as a promotion (though many suspect he felt homesick). His dish consisted of cooked-then-chilled shrimp served in a six-ounce tulip sundae glass with a lemon wedge and spicy cocktail sauce of ketchup, Tabasco, Worcestershire, and lemon.

It caught on instantly, leading to the Golden Gate making it a permanent dish. People visited from all over the world to eat the shrimp cocktail because it was simple, inexpensive (for seafood at the time), yet elegant. Because of its acclaim at the Golden Gate, it became the most popular appetizer in the US from the mid '60s until the late '80s. At the height of its fame, the Golden Gate sold as many as 2,000 shrimp cocktails a day. Even today, Las Vegas still goes through over 60,000 pounds of shrimp each day.

While the Golden Gate has stopped selling its shrimp cocktail, its sister resort, Circa Las Vegas, now sells the original recipe at Saginaw's Delicatessen. Saginaw's is named for and run by Paul Saginaw, an Ann Arbor restaurateur. The delicatessen is a mix of a warm, inviting deli and vintage Vegas style. Open 24 hours, it offers gigantic classic deli sandwiches like a Reuben, tuna melt, and pastrami; hearty dinners like pot roast, meatloaf, and chicken pot pie… and the shrimp cocktail recipe that started it all.

Address 8 Fremont Street, Las Vegas, NV 89101, +1 (702) 726-5506, www.circalasvegas.com/drink-dine/saginaws-delicatessen | Getting there Deuce on the Strip Bus to Carson after Casino Center or Downtown Loop Bus to Fremont Street Experience | Hours Accessible 24 hours | Tip Visit the site where the shrimp cocktail became famous at the Golden Gate Hotel & Casino, which includes a plaque on Fremont Street marking the location of the first telephone in the city of Las Vegas (1 Fremont Street, www.goldengatecasino.com).

83 Sahara West Library

Free art gallery in a local library

The Clark County Library District has 25 branches and serves 1.7 million people across 8,000 square miles, an area larger than the state of Connecticut. With over 3.58 million items in the collection (20 times the number of slot machines in Las Vegas), the Library District is among the top public libraries in the US by size, circulation, and visits. While many of the branches across Las Vegas deserve a mention, the Sahara West branch in Summerlin is the largest library branch in the Library District at over 122,000 square feet.

The exterior of Sahara West Library, designed by the architecture firm Meyer, Scherer & Rockcastle, looks less like your local library and more like a modern concert venue or event hall. But what really sets this location apart is the three art galleries located within the facility that showcase exhibits from local and regional artists.

Because Las Vegas is one of the few major cities in the US without a central art museum, small galleries are essential for displaying art and design. The galleries in the libraries, like at Sahara West, are vital resources to make art accessible, and to enable students, families, and senior citizens to experience art in their own neighborhoods without having to travel to the Strip or Arts District. Darren Johnson, Library District Gallery Services Manager, says, "Art in libraries gives more community ownership and removes some of the stigmas of art elitism that might overwise deter the art curious."

Sahara West's three galleries total over 6,000 feet and include the Studio, the East Gallery, and the West Gallery. The galleries rotate regularly with over 15 exhibits each year, offering regular chances to experience new forms of art like sketches, photography, sculpture, and abstract painting from primarily local artists, or those more well known, like Joseph Beuys, Elizabeth Catlett, and Hale Woodruff.

Address 9600 W Sahara Avenue, Las Vegas, NV 89117, +1 (702) 507-3630, www.thelibrarydistrict.org/locations/SW | Getting there SX-B Sahara Express Bus to Sahara after Grand Canyon | Hours Mon–Thu 10am–8pm, Fri–Sun 10am–6pm | Tip Make your way to East Las Vegas Library for even more art, but also to experience its innovative sound booths and recording studios available for library card holders (2851 E Bonanza Road, www.thelibrarydistrict.org/locations/ev).

84_The Sand Dollar Lounge

Iconic dive bar with live music and killer cocktails

From the outside, The Sand Dollar Lounge doesn't look like much. Found on the ground floor of an aging strip mall, only a relatively small sign indicates there is a music venue behind the dark front doors. But inside is one of the most renowned live music venues in the city. First opened in 1976, as The Sand Dollar Blues Room, it was an ocean-themed industry bar, open late for hospitality workers heading home from the Strip. Called "local Vegas' favorite end-up-there spot" by *Las Vegas Weekly*, it featured gambling, cheap drinks, and great music. Over its 30-year original run, musicians like B. B. King, Mick Jagger, and Muddy Waters would stop by when in town.

After a short closure, it was reopened in 2009: "The spirit of live music in Las Vegas unwilling to fade away… the ghosts in the bar would not die," as it says on the website. Now honoring the history and tradition of the iconic venue, The Sand Dollar Lounge is a hotspot for live music, with performances by members of The Who, The Marshall Tucker Band, Ween, and Blues Traveler, among others. The bar's dedication to featuring talent of the highest standard helped it secure a spot in the Blues Hall of Fame for Outstanding Venue by the Las Vegas Blues Society.

Current owners Anthony Jamison and Nathan Grates are focused on honoring the bar's rich history while breathing new life into this once-beloved spot. Jamison describes The Sand Dollar as the best of both worlds. "It has that classic dive bar, rock-and-roll vibe mixed with the elevated experience of high-end cocktails you'd usually find at upscale spots on the Strip," he says. But what's even better? Their "killer cocktails" (as *Eater Las Vegas* calls them) that are worthy of the best cocktail spots on the Strip are all at dive-bar prices. This dedication to staying grounded in your roots while adapting to new tastes is no doubt reflected in its renewed success.

Address 3355 Spring Mountain Road, Las Vegas, NV 89102, +1 (702) 485-5401, www.thesanddollarlv.com, info@thesanddollarlv.com | Getting there Bus 203 to WB Spring Mountain before Polaris or EB Spring Mountain after Polaris | Hours Mon–Sat 4pm–4am, Sun 8pm–4am | Tip For another dive bar, this time mixed with a sports pub, drop into Moondoggies (3240 Arville Street, www.moondoggiesbar.com).

85_The Scotch 80s

Unaltered mid-century modern neighborhood

Wedged between Charleston Boulevard, Rancho Drive, and I-15 is the Scotch 80s, an upscale residential neighborhood that many associate with "old Las Vegas," because of its large lots, spacious homes, and mid-century modern architecture. It is one of the most exclusive older neighborhoods in Las Vegas and holds some of the most expensive homes in the valley. Many notable residents have called this area home, including Jerry Lewis, Mayor Oscar Goodman, Sammy Davis Jr., Howard Hughes, Steve Wynn, and Nicolas Cage.

How the neighborhood got its name is often disputed. Historian Lynn Zook claims the name came when the first mayor of Las Vegas, Peter Buol, met a Scotsman, Sir John Murray, who agreed to fund an 80-acre development in the blossoming Las Vegas. However, when Great Britain entered WWI, there was a ban on all exported assets, and the development was scrapped. But the name stuck.

Driving around the Scotch 80s, even when viewing Teslas, Land Rovers, and BMWs sitting in the large driveways, feels like stepping back in time to before stones replaced grass in front yards and developers created cookie-cutter homes in various shades of beige.

One resident of the Scotch 80s said the neighborhood is in the perfect location, "10 minutes from everywhere." And while the valley has expanded considerably since this statement was made, it's still fairly accurate. Residents can reach most major attractions like Fremont Street, the Strip, and Spring Mountain Road in about 10 minutes. Many homes also have an unobstructed view of The Strat, an iconic bit of Las Vegas that seems fitting amongst the clean and simple lines of the neighborhood's homes. Viewing this area makes you nostalgic for a possibly simpler time in history, with homes full of character in a fast-growing and eclectic city, even if you weren't alive then.

Address Southwest of the intersection of Charleston Boulevard and Rancho Drive, Las Vegas, NV 89102 | Getting there Bus 206 to Charleston after Shadow | Hours Unrestricted | Tip Continue the tour of mid-century modern homes in Paradise Palms, Vegas' first master-planned community, south of Golden Arrow Drive, north of Viking Road, west of Eastern Avenue, and east of Algonquin, Oneida, and La Canada Streets (www.paradisepalmslasvegas.org).

86_Seven Magic Mountains

Dayglow rock pillars in the Nevada desert

The red-brown mountains encircling Las Vegas are almost as distinctive as the neon-covered Strip. But along Interstate 15 heading toward California, motorists can see a remarkable rock formation that seems to marry the two. *Seven Magic Mountains*, created by Swiss-born Italian artist Ugo Rondinone, consists of seven pillars between 30 and 35 feet high of large neon-colored boulders. Opened in 2016 in collaboration with the Nevada Museum of Art, these locally sourced boulders are painted pinks, purples, blacks, blues, yellows, and greens.

The design was created to contrast with the natural landscape of nearby Jean Dry Lake and the surrounding mountains. The location was chosen, according to Rondinone, because it is physically and symbolically halfway between the natural and the artificial, referencing the natural dry lake bed and mountains and the artificial Interstate highway. Strolling among the pillars, observing the neon colors, the distant desert mountains, and listening to the rush of traffic all deeply capture Rodinone's message.

The installation is not far from where Jean Tinguely (1925–1991) created legendary land art works in the 1960s, which even more adds to the mystique of the piece. Tinguely, also a Swiss artist, created *Study for an End of the World No. 2* in 1962 at Jean Dry Lake Bed. This installation was a self-destructing array of sculptural pieces composed mostly of trash recovered from a nearby landfill in Las Vegas, as a criticism of consumer culture.

Much like Tinguely, Rondinone uses *Seven Magic Mountains* as a critique of the "simulacra of destinations like Las Vegas." Rondinone's work has been featured, among other places, in Paris, Yokohama, New York, and Liverpool. Much of his work is in stone, with giant pillar-like structures in a similar style to *Seven Magic Mountains*.

Address Las Vegas Boulevard South, between Erie and Jean, Las Vegas, NV 89054, +1 (702) 381-5182, www.sevenmagicmountains.com | Getting there By car, take 1-15 South to Sloan Road (exit 25), take Las Vegas Boulevard south approximately seven miles | Hours Unrestricted | Tip Visit nearby Jean Dry Lake Bed for off-highway vehicle adventures (Sloan, NV 89054, www.blm.gov/visit/dispersed-jeanroach-dry-lakes).

87 Siegfried and Roy Estate

Former home of the famed illusionist duo

Siegfried and Roy, who *The Atlantic* called the "most famous magicians since Houdini," brought an estimated 800,000 people annually to Vegas for their world-famous show at The Mirage, which ran from 1990 to 2003. Siegfried Fischbacher and Roy Horn were born in Germany in 1939 and 1944, respectively. The two met in 1957 while working on board the German cruise ship TS *Bremen*. Siegfried was performing magic tricks for guests when Roy offered him his stowaway cheetah to use as part of his act.

They went on to perform in European nightclubs before getting their big break, heading to Las Vegas in 1967 to perform at the Tropicana for the long-running musical revue, *Les Folies Bergere*. They did stints at the Stardust's *Lido de Paris* and the Frontier's *Beyond Belief* before they began their headliner act at the newly opened The Mirage.

The pair lived at the "Jungle Palace," with their free-roaming lions and iconic white tigers (at one time as many as 55 tigers and 16 lions) from 1982 until their deaths in 2020 and 2021. The property, which consists of an 8,750-square-foot main house, separate casita, cabana and pool, two detached studios, and three guest houses, is in a surprisingly ordinary neighborhood near the Las Vegas Country Club. Featuring a white façade that some liken to an adobe castle and a metal gate inlaid with the letters SR, it is an extravagant building that reflects their flamboyant personalities.

Today, the home is owned by George and Brett Carden, the father-son owners of the Carden International Circus. George, who had personally known the magicians thanks to his work with exotic circus animals, wanted to ensure the estate's preservation. "What we would like to do is preserve it for people to make it a shrine for them basically – a piece of history of Las Vegas that's not torn down," Brett told the *Las Vegas Review-Journal*. "It's part of Las Vegas."

Address 1639 Valley Drive, Las Vegas, NV 89108 | Getting there Bus 209 to Vegas after Valley | Hours Viewable from the outside only | Tip For another over-the-top home, visit the Graffiti Mansion for its ever-changing façade that might look like the Barbie Dreamhouse, a Christmas gingerbread house, or an infinite number of designs depending on the artist(s) who have currently taken control of the home (2101 S Pioneer Way, www.graffitimansion.com/graffiti-artists).

88_Sigma Derby

Play the analog table game with its own Facebook page

For many gamblers, nothing will beat the nostalgic games. One such game is the Sigma Derby, an electro-mechanical horse-race table game. Created in 1985 by Japanese manufacturer Sigma Game Inc., up to ten players can place bets on the mechanical five horses to guess who will come in first and second. Once a popular game found in almost every casino throughout the '80s and '90s (like at the Luxor with camels instead of horses and Caesars Palace with chariots), only two of the original games remain: one in Atlantic City and one at The D Las Vegas.

While newer versions have sprouted up with digital screens (including one directly across from this original), the classic analog games remain a favorite of die-hard bettors who love the old-school mechanisms and using one of the few games you can still play with quarters. No dollar bills or players cards here. And when you cash out, there's the iconic and distinctive sound of quarters pouring into the metal hopper that will take gamblers back to the heyday of Vegas gaming.

People come from all over the world to play the retro design. According to the Slot Director, Allen Randal, the Derby is by far The D's most popular game and it even has its own Facebook page. "What makes it popular is the camaraderie and the nostalgic feel that it gives you, playing something that old... I've been here at four in the morning and heard crowds just going crazy." And at more popular times it's difficult to get a seat at the table.

The D owner Derek Stevens is a long-time lover of the Sigma Derby game. He first played one at the Dunes in the '80s on his first visit to Vegas. "You're playing real money, as much as you're playing quarters, so there's an element of authenticity about the game that is pretty special," he told *Atlas Obscura*. "I always loved it, I always thought it was going to work."

Address 301 Fremont Street, Las Vegas, NV 89101, +1 (702) 388-2400, www.thed.com | Getting there Deuce on the Strip Bus to Carson after Casino Center or Downtown Loop Bus to Fremont Street Experience | Hours Accessible 24 hours | Tip Visit Slots-A-Fun at Circus Circus to play some of the last remaining coin-operating slots in Vegas (2880 Las Vegas Boulevard South, www.circuscircus.com/casino-1/slots-fun).

89 Silver State Horseback Riding Tours

Escape the city with calm horses on the trail

Nevada's nickname might be the Silver State, but according to the Bureau of Land Management, it could also be the Wild Horse and Burro State. Nearly half of the nation's wild horses and burros roam Nevada's public lands, like nearby Red Rock Canyon and the Spring Mountains. Horseback riding is an authentic way to experience this heritage and connect with the landscapes where these animals still thrive.

Silver State Horseback Riding Tours has been bringing riders out to experience Nevada's beauty on horseback since 2008. Unlike other tour companies that use donkeys or mules, Silver State exclusively uses horses and prioritizes their well-being by ensuring they are never overworked. Many of the herd are rescues, like guest favorites Eve and Adam, rehabilitated from neglect or saved from slaughter to become gentle trail companions. Others have impressive résumés: Trigger has appeared in magazines and commercials, and been filmed for ESPN's UFC show; Miraya is a favorite for weddings, photoshoots, and music videos; and Eagle has starred in music videos, a Caesars Palace commercial, and *America's Got Talent*. Despite their fame, all are safe, calm trail horses matched to riders by weight and skill level.

From November to May, riders explore Lake Mead's Rainbow Gardens with red rock formations reminiscent of the Grand Canyon, an inactive volcano, and native desert animals like jackrabbits, ground squirrels, and bighorn sheep. In summer, tours move to Mount Charleston's pine forests and alpine meadows, a cool escape from the oppressive temperatures, where deer, wild donkeys, and ancient bristlecone pines are common sights. With morning rides, sunset treks, and barbecue dinner tour options, each offers a chance to leave the city and experience the quiet beauty of southern Nevada on horseback.

Address Sawmill Trailhead, Sawmill Dayuse Loop A Road, Las Vegas, NV 89166, +1 (702) 714-1477, www.silverstatetour.com, silverstatetours@gmail.com | Getting there By car, take US 95 N towards Indian Springs, turn left onto NV-156 S for 13 miles and then turn right onto Sawmill Dayuse Loop A Road | Hours Check website for tour schedule and to book | Tip From native animals to exotic, take a camel ride out in the desert with Camel Safari (2725 River Cliff Road, Bunkerville, www.camelsafari.com, +1 (800) 836-4036).

90 The Simpson House

Beloved cartoon home in a Las Vegas suburb

Red Bark Lane in Henderson's South Valley Ranch area is home to beige stucco houses typical in the valley. But eagle-eyed fans will recognize the features of number 712 as those of the Simpsons' fictional home in Springfield. The replica was built in 1997 to be raffled off during a joint promotional contest with Fox and Pepsi to create buzz for lackluster sales and waning interest in the show.

Developers watched over 100 episodes to capture every detail, from bay windows, the arched front door, and the fireplace (unnecessary in Vegas) to the famous couch, Duff beer in the fridge, and Snowball II's cat dish.

People entered the contest by buying Pepsi products, collecting game pieces, and then tuning in on September 21 to watch "The City of New York vs. Homer Simpson" to see if their number appeared on screen. When no one claimed the prize, Pepsi was forced to draw a random game piece that belonged to Barbara Howard, a 56-year-old retired factory worker from Richmond, Kentucky. She opted for the $75,000 cash prize instead of the house.

Fox had no choice but to repaint the home in muted colors and put it up for sale. It sat on the market for over three years with 24-hour security, though multiple props managed to go missing. In 2001, Danielle and her family (who don't wish to share their last name) bought the home "as is" – though they did redecorate it to their own taste – and have remained its only owners. Even though the stunt ended in a bit of a fizzle, it did garner enough attention to help *The Simpsons* through a slump: it is now the longest-running US TV show in history. It has enough dedicated fans to still search out the strange real-life replica of the cartoon home. While Danielle doesn't mind people stopping to admire her home, some intrusive fans try to enter the property or peer through the windows, which understandably causes distress for her and her family.

Address 712 Red Bark Lane, Henderson, NV 89011 | Getting there BHX-B Boulder Highway Express to Boulder after Galleria | Hours Viewable from the outside only; please bear in mind this is a private property, and respect the family's privacy | Tip See the exterior of Casa de Shenandoah, the one-time home and museum of "Mr. Las Vegas," Wayne Newton (3310 Sunset Road).

91 Skyfall Panoramic Bar & Lounge

Elegant bar with a surprising view

Thanks to its eclectic blend of extravagant and grandiose buildings, the Las Vegas Strip is one of the world's most famous and recognizable streets. While almost every venue along Las Vegas Boulevard has at least one viewing location to allow guests to take in the famous cityscape, the Skyfall Panoramic Bar & Lounge, found on the 64th floor of the W Las Vegas, has one of the greatest views of the Strip, with many calling it the best in the entire city.

The city skyline and the surrounding neighborhoods can be seen from inside the lounge, thanks to its floor-to-ceiling windows, or from the elegant outside patio. The 360-degree views show the entire Las Vegas Valley, but thanks to the W's position at the south end of the Strip, the iconic street can be seen in one glance, including the nearby Luxor all the way to the distant Strat. But the most surprising views come from inside the bathrooms. Each private bathroom cubicle has a floor-to-ceiling window that gives you a view of the South Strip while you complete your business. This unbelievable view is a playful "secret" that makes Skyfall so special and intriguing.

Aside from the views, Skyfall is known for its elegant adult-only atmosphere with a casual dress code (think cocktail party) and its fabulous cocktails. The varied menu was created in collaboration with the James Beard Award-winning and Michelin-starred chef Alain Ducasse. With names like "After Hours," "Rosebud," and "Feathered Friend," the drinks are fun and playful, what they call "the intersection of fine dining and contemporary cocktail culture." Regularly ranked as one of the top bars in Las Vegas, Skyfall deserves a stop for a cocktail and bar nibbles with a staggering view.

Address 3940 Las Vegas Boulevard South, Las Vegas, NV 89119, +1 (877) 632-5400, www.wlasvegas.mgmresorts.com/en/nightlife/skyfall-lounge.html | **Getting there** Deuce on the Strip Bus to Mandalay Bay (Southbound) or Luxor/Mandalay Bay (Northbound) | **Hours** Daily 5pm–midnight | **Tip** For a view from the opposite end of the Strip, make your way to The Strat. Eat at its revolving Top of the World restaurant, or try one of its thrill rides on top of the tallest freestanding tower in the US (42000 Las Vegas Boulevard South, www.thestrat.com).

92 Sloan Canyon Petroglyph Site

Hike to Archaic era petroglyphs

Just south of Las Vegas is the Sloan Canyon National Conservation Area (NCA), a 48,438-acre desert sanctuary with unique geologic features and cultural resources. Sloan Canyon NCA was designated by Congress in November 2002 to protect a portion of Southern Nevada's Mojave Desert, including Sweetwater River and the North McCullough Wilderness Area, which are home to jackrabbits, kit foxes, desert kangaroo rats, chuckwalla lizards, bobcats, roadrunners, and mountain lions.

The main landmark of the area is the Sloan Canyon Petroglyph Site, which the Bureau of Land Management calls one of the most important cultural resources in Southern Nevada. The site is home to more than 300 rock art panels called petroglyphs with 1,700 individual design elements created by native cultures from the Archaic to historic era (about 8,500 B.C. to A.D. 1670). The petroglyphs at Sloan Canyon document the presence of local indigenous tribes, including the Southern Paiute, Puebloan, and Patayan peoples. The figures, which are etched into the weathered patina of the dark volcanic rocks, depict an ancient cross-country route across the mountains: up a canyon, over a divide, and down a valley to the south with images of people, animals, hunt scenes, and geometric shapes.

The best way to visit the petroglyphs is from the aptly named Petroglyph Canyon Trail, a 4.1-mile easy-to-moderate loop trail that leaves from the Visitor Center. Most of the rock art is concentrated in a 500-foot stretch of canyon along a stony streambed with many images easily visible, though some require a little more exploration and a keen eye. But remember, don't climb on, touch, or otherwise disturb any of these centuries-old artworks, which many work extremely hard to preserve for us and future generations.

Address 2998 Nawghaw Poa Road, Henderson, NV 89044, +1 (725) 233-6339, www.blm.gov | Getting there By car, take I-15 South to Exit 25 to Sloan Road, then turn onto Nawghaw Poa Road | Hours Daily 8:30am–4:30pm | Tip Pay a visit to Avi Kwa Ame National Monument, also called Spirit Mountain, considered to be one of the most sacred places on Earth by the Mojave, Chemehuevi, and some Southern Paiute people (NV-163, Laughlin, www.blm.gov/avi-kwa-ame-national-monument).

93_Slot Car City

Nostalgic haven for slot car enthusiasts

Slot car racing, which features 1:24 or 1:32-scale miniature motorized vehicles, is an exciting hobby that blends model-building and high-speed competition. Hobbyists can customize their cars by swapping out motors, tires, and gears to enhance performance, and then paint them to replicate real-life vehicles or showcase imaginative designs. The small electric cars are then raced, guided by grooves in large, slanting tracks. It's a fun pastime that draws in both young hobbyists and dedicated collectors, offering a mix of speed, skill, and creativity.

The hobby was massively popular in the 1960s, quickly becoming a national craze with over 3,000 public tracks across the US at its peak.

However, by the 1970s, interest in the activity had declined. Possibly because of the rising interest in video games and home entertainment, many tracks closed. Today, only a handful of venues keep the tradition alive. One such place is Slot Car City in the Westland Fair Plaza. It's Nevada's only slot car venue, preserving this vintage pastime for hundreds of enthusiasts. Open since 1993, it is the cornerstone of the local racing community, hosting regular events, including weekly races and special series that often feature up to 40 participants each session.

Slot Car City is home to two indoor eight-lane high-speed tracks, each stretching over 140 feet. These huge, winding tracks are the centerpieces of the shop, filling the space and drawing in both racers and casual watchers to see the fast-paced events. There is also an extensive retail space for hobbyists to purchase or rent cars and parts to incorporate into their builds.

But Slot Car City is more than just a place to race miniature cars. It's a place where skill meets nostalgia, where generations connect through a shared passion, and a chance to slow down, focus, and find joy in the details away from the fast-paced digital world.

Address 1271 S Decatur Boulevard, Las Vegas, NV 89102, +1 (702) 438-1760, www.slotcarcity.com, mickyvegas@aol.com | Getting there Bus 103 to Decatur after Faircenter or Decatur after Charleston | Hours Tue, Thu & Fri 5–10pm, Sat noon–10pm, Sun noon–9pm | Tip Check out another hobby store, Friendly Hobbies, for supplies for model aircraft and cars (3616 N Rancho Drive, www.friendlyhobbies.com).

94 The Smelly Bar

Take home a whiff of your favorite Vegas resort

Scent marketing is used by businesses, especially in commercial hubs like Las Vegas, to enhance the overall experience and influence customer behavior. All of the prominent hotels and casinos in the city use distinctive scents that often stick with people long after they've visited. For those looking to replicate some of their favorites, Aroma Retail is the place to go.

This Environmental Scenting Company is just a short drive from the Strip. While it has over 100 scents like autumn bonfire, warm bread, candy shop, and fresh linen, some of its most popular scents are from the Places and Resorts collections.

Using the exact fragrances used by the casinos and hotels (most of which were designed by Aroma Retail's CEO), it has created a way for you to take home a piece of Las Vegas. Choosing from resorts like the Cromwell, Venetian, Caesars Palace, or the Cosmopolitan, you can scent your home or office to match your favorite.

The Smelly Bar, right at the front of its shop, is the perfect place to sample scents to find the ones you'd like to surround yourself with. This immersive experience takes visitors on a scent journey led by a knowledgeable sales associate. Answer questions about your preferences and test dozens of scents from the quaint amber bottles to discover your perfect fragrance. Its pure-grade fragrance oils are free of synthetic toxins and volatile compounds, making them safe for all people, pets, and locations.

Fragrance blending, production of oils, and manufacturing of all of its other products (diffusers, scent machines, soy wax candles) happen in its 13,000-square-foot factory just next to the Smelly Bar. Whether looking for a small diffuser for your desk or a built-in scent machine like the big businesses, a trip to the Smelly Bar is a must if you're a fan of home fragrance or you're looking to take a piece of the Vegas experience home.

Address 5525 S Valley View Boulevard, Las Vegas, NV 89118, +1 (702) 780-7370, www.aromaretail.com, care@aromaretail.com | Getting there Bus 104 to Valley View before Diablo | Hours Mon–Fri 10am–4pm | Tip Visit the Lip Lab to create personalized, one-of-a-kind lipsticks (3200 Las Vegas Boulevard South, www.liplab.com).

95_Snappy's

Retro Americana in an ever-evolving city

In a city hell-bent on the newest, biggest, and brightest, Snappy's takes it old-school with its combination drive-in theater and burger joint. Drive-ins were an essential part of the American experience, with over 4,000 theaters across the US in the late 1950s. That number has dwindled to an estimated 300 remaining nationwide. Snappy's opened in 2020, replicating the classic drive-in experience and adding another American classic, the fast food burger.

Owner Jon Basso, known around the valley for his outlandish restaurants, explains that he loves everything retro: the old movies, the burgers, and the drive-ins. "It's all about being classic. That's why I opened this. Because people need this," he told *Las Vegas Morning Blend*. "This is almost extinct from the world we live in today."

Snappy's parking lot sits in front of a large outdoor screen. Day and night they show rom-coms, sci-fi, horror, classics that rotate weekly. Snappy's small menu, which you order from the drive-thru line before claiming your spot in front of the screen, is filled with the classics: burgers, fries, grilled cheese, popcorn, candy, and soda. Everything you would want while relaxing in your car and watching a movie. The burgers are juicy, greasy (an essential for Jon) Angus beef with lettuce, tomato, pickles, American cheese, and jalapeños (if you ask for them "Extra Snappy").

For adults, this is a place for nostalgia, whereas younger generations marvel at the novelty of eating their food in their car while watching a movie on the big screen. Jon says he loves seeing the light in children's eyes. He grew up with the drive-in and he wishes more still existed today. "That's the whole reason I got involved with Snappy's," Jon went on. "I just want people to enjoy a burger, have a movie, slow down life a little bit." And Snappy's is just the place to do that.

Address 101 N Decatur Boulevard, Las Vegas, NV 89107, www.snappys.fun | Getting there Bus 103 to Decatur after Bonanza | Hours Daily 10:30am–11pm | Tip Visit Jon Basso's other restaurant, the bizarre Heart Attack Grill on Fremont for a hospital-themed spot focusing on extremely high-calorie foods (450 Fremont Street, www.heartattackgrill.com).

96 Springs Preserve's Nature Exchange

Kids share nature finds to earn exciting rewards

Home to the Nevada State and Origen Museums, nature trails, botanical gardens, and galleries, the Springs Preserve is a cultural institution. The 180-acre property is located at the site of the Las Vegas Springs, a natural oasis that inspired the city's name: Las Vegas means "The Meadows" in Spanish. The Preserve is an essential visit for locals and visitors alike to learn about the area's natural history and the city's development, from the early mining days to today's glamorous gaming and entertainment empire.

One incredible interactive feature at the Preserve is its Nature Exchange program. Aimed at kids, it encourages responsible and ethical collecting, allowing "young naturalists" to trade found items like shells, bark, pinecones, rocks, and fossils to earn points. Points can then be redeemed for a new item from the Preserve's collection of dozens of unique items like fossils, giant sea shells, or beautiful amethyst crystals from the local environment and beyond.

Collecting natural objects in their surroundings encourages kids to go out and explore, get into nature, and learn about their environment. "They get a new look to how they see things when they're out in nature," says Chris Sakmar, Naturalist at the Springs Preserve. "Looking for items that are cool they could bring in, and at the same time, developing an interest in science."

Kids can bring in up to five items each visit to collect points based on the uniqueness and quality of the item and any information provided based on research they conduct.

The impact of a program like this can be seen in kids down the road. "Students that were 10 and 12 years old 10 years ago are now in college," Sakmar continued. "Getting scholarships and being rewarded for the interest they had in nature."

Address 333 S Valley View Boulevard, Las Vegas, NV 89107, +1 (725) 822-7700, www.springspreserve.org | Getting there Bus 207 to Meadows after Valley View or Bus 104 to Valley View after Meadows | Hours Check website for seasonal hours | Tip Continue your museum tour at the Las Vegas Natural History Museum for more on history in the Valley and beyond (900 Las Vegas Boulevard North, www.lvnhm.org).

97 St. Thomas Ghost Town

Abandoned town long submerged beneath Lake Mead

During the construction of the Hoover Dam, then the Boulder Dam, the banks of the Colorado River to the north slowly filled with water, eventually creating the sprawling Lake Mead. The Mormon settlement of St. Thomas, once a thriving waypoint between Los Angeles and Salt Lake City at the meeting of the Virgin and Muddy Rivers, slowly disappeared beneath the waters. By the late 1930s, the town was completely submerged. At the height of the lake's capacity, it was more than 60 feet below the surface.

St. Thomas was first founded by Mormon settlers in 1865, believing they were in the Utah/Arizona territories. After officials in Nevada discovered their settlement in 1870, they demanded five years of back taxes, which the Mormons refused to pay, abandoning the settlement. A new group of settlers arrived at the townsite in the 1880s. At the peak of its existence, at least 500 people lived there with a school, grocery store, post office, soda fountain, church, and eventually a few garages for the new invention: the car. However, the town never had indoor plumbing or electricity.

Before the construction of the dam, residents of St. Thomas were told to relocate, with the government reimbursing them for their property. The lake began to fill in 1935 and while most people left, one man, Hugh Lord, refused to leave until the rising water lapped at his front door in 1938. Due to fluctuating water levels, the town resurfaced for short times in 1945 and 1963, and finally in 2012, where it has remained above water since. During the years when the town reemerged from the water, former residents and descendants of the site gathered at the site for reunions. Now managed by the Lake Mead National Recreation Area, the area contains exposed roads, trails, and building foundations that survived under water for nearly 75 years, making the area almost like an Old West Atlantis.

Address Historic St. Thomas Loop Trail Head, Old Saint Thomas Road, Overton, NV 89040, +1 (702) 293-18990, www.nps.gov/lake/learn/nature/st-thomas-nevada.htm | **Getting there** By car, take I-15 North to Exit 75 to Valley of Fire Highway, turn onto Northshore Road, then onto Old Saint Thomas Road | **Hours** Daily dawn–dusk | **Tip** Visit the nearby Lost City Museum to learn about the Pueblo Grande de Nevada civilization and its people (721 S Moapa Valley Boulevard, www.lostcitymuseum.org).

98 Strip Benchmarks

Brass medallions on the legendary neon boulevard

Each day, thousands of people walk the Strip. Between the larger-than-life architectural spectacles, the signature attractions, and the often interesting people-watching, there is so much to draw attention. But just beneath the feet of pedestrians are often overlooked gold medallions embedded into the pavement.

Multiple disc types can be found along the Strip that have different functions depending on their markings. Agencies like the Nevada Department of Transportation, the US Geological Survey, and Clark County Public Works all manage and monitor markers along this route. Some markers are used to monitor the possible changes in the land.

As one of the busiest streets in the world, with an estimated 40 million visitors each year, and constant changes and additions of megaresorts, the land is at risk of shifting. The markers are used to measure any changes in the stability of the ground to ensure adjustments can be made for safety. Other markers are used to aid GPS satellites, ensuring that the Strip, and the valley as a whole, are accurately represented now and in the future.

While committed searchers may have to do some serious sleuthing to find all of these discs, most averagely curious explorers won't have to search hard to find the special Right of Way markers that feature the design of the "Welcome to Las Vegas" sign. These markers, used as survey boundary markers to delineate the public right of way for the Strip, are conveniently placed intermittently along the street.

While, at first, it might feel like looking for a needle in a haystack, they are fairly easy to spot every few blocks. So long as you keep your eyes on the ground like a local and not on all the buildings like a tourist, you're bound to spot some as you traverse one of the busiest streets in the world.

Address Corner of Las Vegas Boulevard South and Paris Drive, Las Vegas, NV 89109 | Getting there Deuce on the Strip Bus to SB Las Vegas at Bellagio/Cosmo or NB Planet Hollywood | Hours Unrestricted | Tip For another type of benchmark, venture out to the Last Spike historical marker, which marks the spot the last railroad spike was placed to connect the rails going from Salt Lake City to Los Angeles in 1905 (Las Vegas Boulevard South, halfway between Jean and Erie, Sloan).

99_The Tank Pool

Take a waterslide through a shark tank

The Tank Pool at the Golden Nugget may seem like your typical Vegas pool: a three-story pool complex with large swimming area, hot tub, poolside bar, private cabanas, adults-only areas, five gaming tables, and waterfalls. Even the 200,000-gallon aquarium directly in the center of the pool, filled with a plethora of sea life, might not seem out of place in a city of over-the-top feats. But looking closer at the tank, you'll notice a one-of-a-kind feature that is the delight of both kids and adults: a clear waterslide going directly through the center of the tank.

The 300-foot slide is completely enclosed with clear plexiglass, allowing swimmers to travel through the center of the tank, getting 360-degree views of the sea life. This includes over 300 sharks, such as blacktip sharks, tiger sharks, sand tiger sharks, zebra sharks, and nurse sharks, as well as stingrays, and hundreds of other exotic fish. Even when not taking the slide, swimmers can hang out in the pool that wraps 360 degrees around the central tank. Sit nearby, submerged in water, while watching the sea life in the aquarium swim by. Kids will also love the large waterfall that makes for fun splashing, doing laps around the circular tank, or hiding out in the "cave" beneath the top deck.

Named as one of the top pools in the world by CNN, the water is heated to 83 degrees all year round, which makes for nice pool temps in the summer and chilly shoulder seasons. The pool area also includes a separate section for the 21-and-up crowd – the Hideout, which includes a bar, cabanas, and daybeds.

The pool is complimentary for hotel guests, but day passes are available. This makes the pool a great place for families with children to escape the summer Vegas heat while giving the kids an even cooler experience of safely "swimming" with sharks and other exotic fish.

Address 129 Fremont Street, Las Vegas, NV 89101, +1 (702) 385-7111, www.goldennugget.com/las-vegas/amenities/h2o-pool | Getting there Deuce on the Strip Bus to Carson after Casino Center | Hours Check website for seasonal hours | Tip For more aquarium fun, visit the Shark Reef Aquarium at Mandalay Bay (3950 Las Vegas Boulevard South, www.mandalaybay.mgmresorts.com/en/entertainment/shark-reef-aquarium.html).

100 Themed Street Names

Quirky addresses inspired by cartoon favorites

Las Vegas is among the fastest growing cities in the country. Between new highways, casinos, sports stadiums, and the homes for all of the new arrivals in town, there's always something new being built in this city. But with the increase in new neighborhoods comes one issue that developers run into: naming their streets. There are only so many presidents, trees, or numbers before you start repeating or creating confusion. To ensure unique and memorable street names, some developers have taken to using well-known names from pop culture. From Pokémon to trains, The Beatles to magic, quirky street names can be found just about anywhere in Vegas.

Near Sandhill and Russell, just east of the airport, you can find *Star Wars* classics like Leia Street, Skywalker Avenue, and Vader Avenue. Near Floyd Lamb Park in the northwest valley, streets can be found called Amtrak Express Avenue, Eurorail Street, Polar Express Court, and for some added fun, Crazy Train Court. But possibly the most well-known collection of street names is in the Pokémon neighborhood. In Henderson, you can find Jigglypuff Place, Squirtle Lane, and Snorlax Lane.

Andrea Miller, Project Manager at Harmony Homes, a California development company, is responsible for the Pokémon-inspired names in the Serenity Place development, which opened in 2023. Miller was at a loss for what to name the new streets, so she took some inspiration from her children's interest in Pokémon. She said she hoped the names would be memorable and put a smile on people's faces. Her favorite street name? Jigglypuff. She says "When I hear Jigglypuff, I giggle."

Andrea is also responsible for another well-known collection of street names: The Paw Patrol-inspired streets in North Las Vegas, again getting inspiration from her kids' favorite characters at the time of development.

Address Jigglypuff Place, Henderson, NV 89015 | Getting there Bus 212 to Sunset after Pabco | Hours Unrestricted | Tip Lovers of Las Vegas history can pay a visit to the Strip to find nearby streets dedicated to local legends like Frank Sinatra Drive, Sammy Davis Jr. Drive, and Elvis Presley Boulevard.

101 Tom Devlin's Monster Museum

Exhibits dedicated to horror movie magic

Heading into Boulder City, you'll come across a surprising building surrounded by images of celebrated classic horror movies and objects like Frankenstein's monster, the Swamp Thing, and the Ghostbusters car. This is home to Tom Devlin's Monster Museum. Owner Tom Devlin opened his museum in 2017 to share his art collection with the world and preserve the art and history of special makeup effects. Fans of classic movie monsters will feel right at home in this spooky museum. Chucky, Michael Myers, and the Wolfman can be found side-by-side while you navigate the dimly lit, eerie hallways. Displays near exhibits give information on classic horror characters, films, actors, and directors, paying homage to some of the industry's leaders. It is also home to Devlin's screen-used props, creature suits, and custom pieces representing monsters throughout movie history.

Devlin, a professional special effects makeup artist, has worked on over 160 feature films, including *Club Dread*, *Slaughterhouse on the Hill*, and *The After Dark*. He also appeared as a contestant on the first season of the SyFy show *Face Off*, quickly becoming a fan favorite for his realistic and scary makeup effects. Devlin calls the museum "the mystery house" because it is constantly changing and evolving. He updates the museum about three times a year to ensure that visitors can come back time and again to see new props, costumes, and information about horror movie history and culture.

Tom continues to create creatures for films and provides costumes and prosthetics for photo ops at horror conventions across the country for stars like Tony Todd, Kane Hodder, and Warrington Gillette. In 2022, he debuted his first feature film, *Teddy Told Me To,* which was filmed in the back workshop on the property, based on his *Face Off* character.

Address 1310 Boulder City Parkway, Boulder City, NV 89005, +1 (702) 294-1313, www.tomdevlinsmonstermuseum.com | Getting there Bus 221 to Boulder City Parkway before Juniper | Hours Daily 10am–6pm | Tip For another wild museum attraction, though much more scientifically accurate, visit the Bodies… The Exhibition to view real human bodies that have been meticulously dissected, and preserved through an innovative process (3900 Las Vegas Boulevard South, Las Vegas, www.luxor.mgmresorts.com/en/entertainment/bodies-the-exhibition.html).

102 Tule Springs Ranch

Quickie weddings and quickie divorces

In 1931, the Nevada Legislature passed two bills to help restart economic growth during the Great Depression: one was to legalize gambling, and the other to change the divorce requirements to only a six-week waiting period while adding new grounds for divorce. At this time, most states required a one-year wait while also requiring concrete proof of adultery or abandonment.

People flocked to Nevada, spurring the creation of divorce ranches and the divorce tourism industry. These ranches were essentially retreats for adults where they could swim, fish, take horseback riding lessons, and eat authentic Western cuisine while they established residency. Most of the inhabitants at these ranches were women who, at the time, were typically without full-time jobs (*Mad Men* fans will remember Betty Draper heading to Nevada to get a divorce). While the boom of these ranches started in Reno, Las Vegas ranches, in true Vegas fashion, grew quickly thanks to their celebrity clientele, like Clark Gable's wife, Ria Langham, who gave an exclusive interview to the *Las Vegas Review-Journal*, talking about how great of a vacation she'd had.

The best example of a divorce ranch in the area is Tule Springs at what is now Floyd Lamb Park, which operated from 1948 until the 1960s, when more states liberalized their divorce laws, which quickly ended divorce tourism in Nevada. Very few artifacts of these ranches remain today, but Tule Springs has preserved the structures from the ranch and is listed on the US National Register of Historic Places. Visitors can view the guest house, the duplex, the remains of the swimming pool, a small suspension bridge that once crossed a pond, and stables for horses and farm animals. You can also see the site's collection of peacocks casually walking around the property, or head into the park itself for walking trails, picnic areas, and fishing ponds.

Address 9200 Tule Springs Road, Las Vegas, NV 89131, +1 (702) 229-8100, www.lasvegasnevada.gov/Residents/Parks-Facilities/Floyd-Lamb-Park | Getting there By car, take 95N to Exit 93 at Durango Drive, then turn right on Brent Lane to park entrance | Hours Daily May–Sept 8am–8pm, Oct–Apr 9am–5pm | Tip See more historic buildings from a well-known Las Vegas divorce ranch at Lorenzi Park (3333 W Washington Avenue).

103_Underground Mansion

Enter a luxury Cold War-era subterranean home

Twenty-three feet below Spencer Street is an underground home many have heard of, but never seen. Completed in 1978 by millionaire serial entrepreneur Jerry Henderson, the Underground Mansion is the first luxury underground home ever built. A total of 15,000 square feet, it consists of a 6,000-square foot main home with two bedrooms, three bathrooms, a kitchen, living room, dining room, bar, billiards room, and library, with a small casita just off the main home. The design and furnishings are solidly '70s. From the mirrored walls, the pink silk-walled bathroom, and the retro appliances, it's a step into a bygone era.

The space also contains "outdoor" areas, including a gorgeous pool and artificial trees. All four massive walls are adorned with custom-made murals by artist Jewel Smith, featuring locales important to Henderson and his wife Mary, including Colorado, the Swiss Alps, Suffern, NY, Hollywood, and New Zealand, while the ceiling is dotted with fluorescent stars. This all gives the impression of an outdoor space, a welcome feeling if you're actually unable to leave. In that instance, the Underground Mansion can be completely self-sufficient and sealed off from the outside world.

In the 1950s, architect Jay Swayze created Atomitats – family-friendly shelters that are atomic proof – and built homes that could both shield families from the nuclear fallout feared during the Cold War, and also provide more pragmatic safety from burglars or peeping Toms. Together, Henderson and Swayze pioneered underground living, with Swayze designing an underground home for the 1964 World's Fair. While the concept never caught on (he built four others that no longer exist), "The last Atomitat has so much potential for educational and historical value," says Frankie Lewis, the director of events and business development. "The Underground Mansion is one of the most unique places on Earth."

Address 3970 Spencer Street, Las Vegas, NV 89119, +1 (702) 706-6962, www.undergroundmansion.com, FrankieVegasUnderground@gmail.com | Getting there Bus 212 to Flamingo after Spencer | Hours By appointment only | Tip For more '70s decor, drop into the iconic Peppermill restaurant, featured in films like *Casino* and *Showgirls* (2985 Las Vegas Boulevard South, www.peppermilllasvegas.com).

104 Vegas Theatre Company

The playhouse at the heart of the Arts District

Las Vegas' Arts District, just south of Fremont in the downtown area, is the beating heart of the city where bold murals and street art, eclectic galleries, and hip cafés create a dynamic blend of urban culture and artistic expression. According to the City of Las Vegas, this area "has emerged and grown organically over the last several decades into one of our most celebrated neighborhoods." The Vegas Theatre Company has been there since the beginning. It was started by four UNLV students, who have been part of the city's art scene since 2003 (then called the Cockroach Theatre Company). Located in the Arts Square building since 2013, they have watched the Arts District flourish around them, including their sister theater, Majestic Repertory Theater.

Run by Artist Director Daz Weller, the intimate 80-seat black box theater features new, original productions, like *The House on Watch Hill*, written by Tony Award-winning writers Richard Oberacker and Robert Taylor, which features young local actors in "the captivating tale of friendship, frights, and unexpected twists," and *Abandon*, a horror production written by Jana Wimer, Robert Bullwinkle and Abel Horwitz. With the support of the Nevada Arts Council and the National Endowment for the Arts, they also open their space to "give a home to local creation." Facilitating plays, adult acting workshops, opera, novelty acts, improv, and festivals to allow others to develop and create. Most recently, their partnership with Alchemy Arts Academy, or A3 Youth Theatre, has helped develop theater skills and confidence in young performers.

In addition to their productions, they also feature monthly burlesque shows, pop-up shows where local on-Strip performers workshop new acts, and live comedy events, as well as a free cabaret during First Friday, the Arts District's free monthly event with vendors, music, and local art.

Address 1025 S First Street #110, Las Vegas, NV 89101, +1 (725) 222-9661, www.theatre.vegas, info@theatre.vegas | **Getting there** Deuce on the Strip Bus to Casino Center at Coolidge | **Hours** Check website for show schedule | **Tip** Walk to the nearby Arts Factory, home to over 30 artists and galleries plus small stores, restaurants, and coffee shops all centered around art and creativity (107 E Charleston Boulevard, www.theartsfactorylv.com).

105 Velveteen Rabbit

Indulge in cocktails that redefine the experience

In the heart of the Arts District is a bar with a long reputation for being a trendy and intimate spot to grab a drink. Named the "Best Cocktail Bar" by *Las Vegas Weekly*, Velveteen Rabbit was opened in 2013 by sisters and Las Vegas locals Christina and Pamela Dylag. The sisters created a space to reflect their shared values of creativity, art, and connection. The name Velveteen Rabbit, which any book lover will know, is borrowed from the classic children's book by Margery Williams. But the name is more of a subtle reference, meant to conjure up nostalgia, something well-loved, welcoming, and memorable.

While the exterior is easy to pass by while exploring the lively and local neighborhood, the interior is inviting and warm, what *Las Vegas Weekly* called "a work of art" with bar seating and comfortable Victorian couches in a multitude of colors. Their "Pink Palace" outdoor patio is perfect for warm summer nights, with pink and blue umbrellas and floral murals that transport you into another magical world.

The true star of Velveteen Rabbit is its cocktails, which one patron called "the best alcoholic drinks I've ever tasted." The menu rotates every three to four months and is based around a central theme like "Road Trip" or "Viva Lost Vegas!" with each of the cocktails paying homage to the theme. The "No Sympathy for the Devil" is inspired by *Fear and Loathing in Las Vegas* with marigold-infused rum, crème de mûre, salted walnut syrup, lemon, and walnut bitters. While they do have crowd-favorite cocktails and beers that appeal to everyone, they also have "sleeper hits" as Christina calls them, that do well with cocktail lovers. Like their "North End," a clarified cocktail that emulates a Caprese salad. The bar's award-winning innovative cocktails have a tight grip on patrons, keeping them coming back to experience something new and exciting, yet refined and familiar.

Address 1218 S Main Street, Las Vegas, NV 89104, +1 (702) 685-9645, www.velveteenrabbitlv.com, info@velveteenrabbitlv.com | Getting there Deuce on the Strip Bus to 3rd after Imperial or 3rd before Imperial | Hours Sun–Thu 5pm–midnight, Fri & Sat 5pm–2am | Tip For another cool lounge, visit Más Por Favor in Chinatown for a speakeasy experience (3879 Spring Mountain Road, www.masporfavorlv.com).

106 Vibes DIY Studio

Vegas' top do-it-yourself art studio

Vibes DIY Studio, in the quaint shopping area Village at Centennial Hills, is taking social media by storm and bringing in countless customers to "DIY in style." Vibes DIY specializes in rug tufting, a relatively new DIY obsession to create custom rugs, as well as hand painting and paint pouring. This family-run shop, operated by Marybeth Pagela and her daughter and son-in-law, Cooper and CJ Hayes, began when, like many in 2020, Marybeth and Cooper were looking for ways to stay busy. They fed their creativity by getting into rug tufting. Around that time, Marybeth sought to leave her corporate 9-to-5 to prioritize her health and her family. Taking a leap of faith, they opened Vibes DIY to combine their creative spirit, their new passion for rug tufting, and create a better life balance.

Rug tufting is a relatively easy craft that can be challenging and expensive to get started. But Vibes DIY helps every step of the way by creating your custom template, offering over 90 yarn colors, setting up your frame, providing instruction on the tufting gun, technique, and trimming and backing the finished rug. The project is fun, unique, and perfect for those looking to create custom, functional art for their space.

And like the name suggests, the atmosphere in Vibes is... a vibe. While it's kid-friendly (though some younger teens might find rug tufting difficult), there are plenty of groups that make Vibes their own paint and pour, with BYOB and a fun after-work-drinks atmosphere.

Before Vibes DIY, Las Vegas lacked a creative space for all generations to come and express themselves through art. Though rug tufting has increased in popularity thanks to social media, Vibes remains the only location in all of Nevada to specialize in rug tufting, making it a huge draw for locals and visitors alike to try out the new craft.

Address 7575 Norman Rockwell Lane, Suite 120, Las Vegas, NV 89143, +1 (702) 395-3349, www.vibesdiystudio.com, create@vibesdiystudio.com | Getting there Bus 106 to Farm after Tule Springs | Hours Wed, Thu & Sun noon–7pm, Sat 10am–9pm | Tip Continue your tour of Vegas' art studios with Clay Arts Vegas for classes on wheel throwing and hand building (1353 Arville Street, www.clayartsvegas.com).

107 Viva Las VegaStamps!

Shop with the largest collection of rubber stamps

Viva Las VegaStamps!, found down on East Sahara Avenue, is a one-of-a-kind destination for artists, collectors, and the creatively curious. Calling themselves "America's Rubber Stamp Paradise," the shop is home to one of the largest and most eclectic collections of rubber stamps in the world. With more than 20,000 unique designs, visitors can browse shelves packed with inspiring motifs, from the whimsical to the surreal, the vintage to the downright strange. The ceiling glows with real neon lights while the exterior is adorned with replica "Welcome to Las Vegas" signs fit with the shop's name: an intentional homage to the classic Las Vegas atmosphere envisioned by the shop's founder, Wayne Gartley.

Wayne moved to Las Vegas in the early 1980s and began rubber stamping as a personal hobby. Frustrated by the limited options available, he began creating his own designs, eventually turning his passion into a business. He opened the original Viva Las VegaStamps! store in 1993 and relocated to its current location in 2001. His nephew, Jeff Gartley, took over the business in 2009, maintaining Wayne's vision while continuing to expand the shop's global reach. Today, they ship their stamps around the world and have drawn new attention through viral features on TikTok and Instagram with many craft enthusiasts falling in love with the seemingly endless collection displayed on the floor-to-ceiling shelves.

All stamps are handmade in Vegas, with new designs releasing regularly. Popular patterns include Banksy replicas, the whimsical drawings of Mary Vogel Lozinak, steampunk motifs, holiday icons, and of course iconic Vegas images. While the shop remains a niche destination, it has become a landmark for creatives in Las Vegas with many making trips out simply to visit the shop and standing by (sort of) patiently waiting for new design releases.

Address 1008 E Sahara Avenue, Las Vegas, NV 89104, +1 (702) 836-9118, www.vlvstamps.com, sales@vlvstamps.com | **Getting there** SX-B Bus to Sahara after Commercial Center or Bus 109 to Maryland after St. Louis | **Hours** Mon–Fri 10am–4pm | **Tip** Continue your arts and crafts tour at Desert Art Supplies, "Southern Nevada's Complete Art Store" (2003 E Charleston, www.desertartsupplies.com).

108 Votes for Women Historic Marker

Honoring Las Vegas' role in women's suffrage

Shortly after Las Vegas' incorporation in 1905, a women's group called the Mesquite Club came together to focus on local community improvements. Officially established in 1911 by Delphine Squires, a writer at her husband's newspaper, the *Las Vegas Age*, and "the First Lady of Las Vegas" Helen J. Stewart. Delphine, known as "Mom," (her husband was "Pop") had long been a proponent for the importance of education and women's rights.

Their first project was to create shade trees in the young desert city. They raised money for cottonwood trees, planted them on every lot, and cared for them until they were fully grown. Another notable project was to establish the public library. In 1912, the Mesquite Club was added as a member of the Nevada Federation of Women's Clubs.

The Club's most wide-reaching project, however, was its involvement in Women's suffrage. The Club hosted suffrage speakers such as Charlotte Perkins Gilman, who came from Reno and the capital of Carson City, as well as New York, to give talks on women's legal status and political opportunities. These talks were instrumental in convincing male voters to support votes for women (a resolution that would allow women to vote, as long as current voters – men – agreed). In the November 1914 general election, men voted 3-1 in Clark County to allow women in Nevada to vote in state and local elections.

Today, a plaque is placed near the Historic Fifth Street School, where the Club met until 1915. Sponsored by the William G. Pomeroy Foundation, the marker is part of the National Votes for Women Trail as a project of the National Collaborative for Women's History Sites that has over 200 markers across the country. Unveiled in 2020, the marker honors Delphine Squires for her role in advancing women's rights.

Address 4th Street, between Lewis and Clark Avenues, Las Vegas, NV 89101 | Getting there Deuce on the Strip Bus to Casino Center at Bonneville Transit Center | Hours Unrestricted | Tip Visit one of the Mesquite Club's public events to see what the club is up to today (702 E St Louis Avenue, www.mesquiteclub.com).

109_ Warsaw Ghetto Remembrance Garden

Pieces of Holocaust history in Las Vegas

During World War II, German soldiers forced more than 400,000 Jews into the Warsaw Ghetto, a 1.3-square-mile city enclosed by 10-foot walls topped with barbed wire and broken glass. More than 1,100 ghettos were established in Europe to separate Jewish and non-Jewish communities, and to control the Jewish population with strict rules and hard labor. Paving stones from the Warsaw Ghetto have made their way around the globe, including to the United States Holocaust Memorial Museum in Washington, D.C. The largest collection is now in the Warsaw Ghetto Remembrance Garden at Temple Beth Sholom.

Henry Kronberg, survivor of the Krakow Ghetto and three separate concentration camps, was instrumental in acquiring the stones and creating the garden. Kronberg and Rabbi Felipe Goodman arranged for what they thought would be a dozen or so stones to create their memorial but were shocked to receive more than 200, mainly from Warsaw's Chłodna Street. The circular outdoor garden, just outside the temple, has stones placed in the ground and displayed on the walls. In the center is a stone table with an etched map of the Warsaw Ghetto. Soft music can be heard, such as a score by Władysław Szpilman, whose experiences in Warsaw inspired the film *The Pianist*.

Kronberg's wife, Lillian, was a survivor of the Warsaw Ghetto as well as Auschwitz and Bergen-Belsen concentration camps. "If the stones could talk, they would tell you what we went through," Lillian told the *Las Vegas Sun* during construction. Kronberg, Edyth Katz, and Judith Mack are also responsible for creating the Holocaust Resource Library, a multi-room library at the temple, housing hundreds of fiction, nonfiction, and reference materials on the Holocaust, WWII, and prejudice of any form. Open to the public, both the library and garden are reminders and sources of information on tragic time in history.

Address 10700 Havenwood Lane, Las Vegas, NV 89135, +1 (702) 804-1333, www.bethsholomlv.org, info@bethsholomlv.org | Getting there Bus 203 to Desert Inn before Town Center or Sahara after Town Center | Hours By appointment only | Tip See King David Holocaust Memorial for the largest memorial in Las Vegas dedicated to the Holocaust (2697 E Eldorado Lane).

110_Water Street District

Henderson's historic street, brought back to life

When it comes to cities in Southern Nevada, Las Vegas dominates the story. But the history of Henderson, which in itself is the second largest city in the state, is just as interesting. The Basic Magnesium plant opened in what is now Henderson in 1941. The plant grew exponentially after the US joined the Second World War, bringing thousands of jobs to the new town. It's said that Henderson was "born in America's defense" as it was a key site for the magnesium production used in airplane parts and ammunition. Much like the Hoover Dam before it, a townsite, called Basic Townsite, was created to house the more than 15,000 workers and their families in the then-remote town. This is what would eventually become the city of Henderson when it was incorporated in 1953.

Water Street was where "Henderson's heart once beat" according to the city's Henderson Historical Walking Tour. Named for the pipeline running the length of the street (which fed the plant), it was home to the City Hall Plaza, the one-room schoolhouse, and many of the town's blossoming businesses. Mark S. Schulman's grocery store was the first business to inhabit Henderson's "Strip."

Today, Water Street is having a revival, thanks to the City of Henderson Redevelopment Agency. Dozens of businesses like the popular Public Works Coffee Bar, Sticks Tavern, The Pass Casino, Mojave Brewing Company, and Chef Flemming's Bake Shop now inhabit the one-mile street, looking to bring back the charm of the local shopping district the city was lacking. And that small-town feel, mixed with upscale and trendy businesses, is bringing the community back to the downtown area.

Water Street feels like a community in itself, with businesses coexisting and looking to build the street as a whole. As John Griffith of Mojave Brewing Company said, "When we walk down the street we see friends and family rather than strangers."

Address 280 S Water Street, Henderson, NV 89015, +1 (702) 267-1515, www.waterstreetdistrict.com, cohredevelopment@cityofhenderson.com | Getting there BHX-B Boulder Highway Express to Boulder after Basic | Hours Unrestricted from the outside, check websites for business hours | Tip Visit the Clark County Museum to see a real Henderson townsite home (as well as homes from the Boulder Dam project) and learn more about Clark County's early settlements (1830 S Boulder Highway, Henderson, www.clarkcountynv.gov).

111_Wax Trax Records

Local record shop bursting at the seams

Stepping inside Wax Trax is like entering a vinyl collector's fever dream. Every square inch of space across three floors of a converted house is taken up by a labyrinth of makeshift shelves, meticulously categorized by genre then alphabetized. Even the bathroom is chock-full of records. Owner Rich Rosen says he has "at least a million" records in his shop, with plenty more in his warehouse. With everything from rock and roll and R&B to jazz and doo-wop, it's hard to imagine there's a record that exists that can't be found at Wax Trax, though Rich says there are a few he's still searching for. Wax Trax is "for serious buyers and collectors," says one customer. "It holds some of the most impossibly hard-to-find records."

But Rich himself is a draw for many. Now in his 80s, he has been collecting records for over 60 years. He owned shops in New York and Pennsylvania before opening up Wax Trax in Vegas in 1998. Rich is a fount of knowledge about records and music, and his unapologetically gruff personality is reflected in online reviews (which range from glowing to scathing). But Rich doesn't mind. In an interview with the *Las Vegas Review-Journal* in 2017, he said what makes up for the bad reviews is Elton's people. That would be Elton John. Elton's team came in looking for a gift. "Then I get a call saying that Elton would like to come to the store. Now, before he does a show, he comes here, sits there for three hours. I keep handing him records, and he takes what he wants" (on his first visit, he bought over 200). And Elton, himself, called Wax Trax an "Aladdin's cave," in an interview with British radio DJ Paul Gambaccini in 2017.

Also unique to the store is the absence of price tags. If you find a record you like, they'll check the market value at the register, something that Rich says he'll never change, though many people hate it. "That's old-school to me," he says.

Address 2909 S Decatur Boulevard, Las Vegas, NV 89102, +1 (702) 362-4300, www.waxtraxonline.com, waxtraxlv@gmail.com | Getting there Bus 103 to Decatur after Pennwood or Decatur before Edna | Hours Daily 10am–3pm | Tip Continue your browsing with a stop at The Analog Dope store, a combination book/record store with a focus on Black culture, African diaspora, and POC (205 E Colorado Avenue, www.analogdope.com).

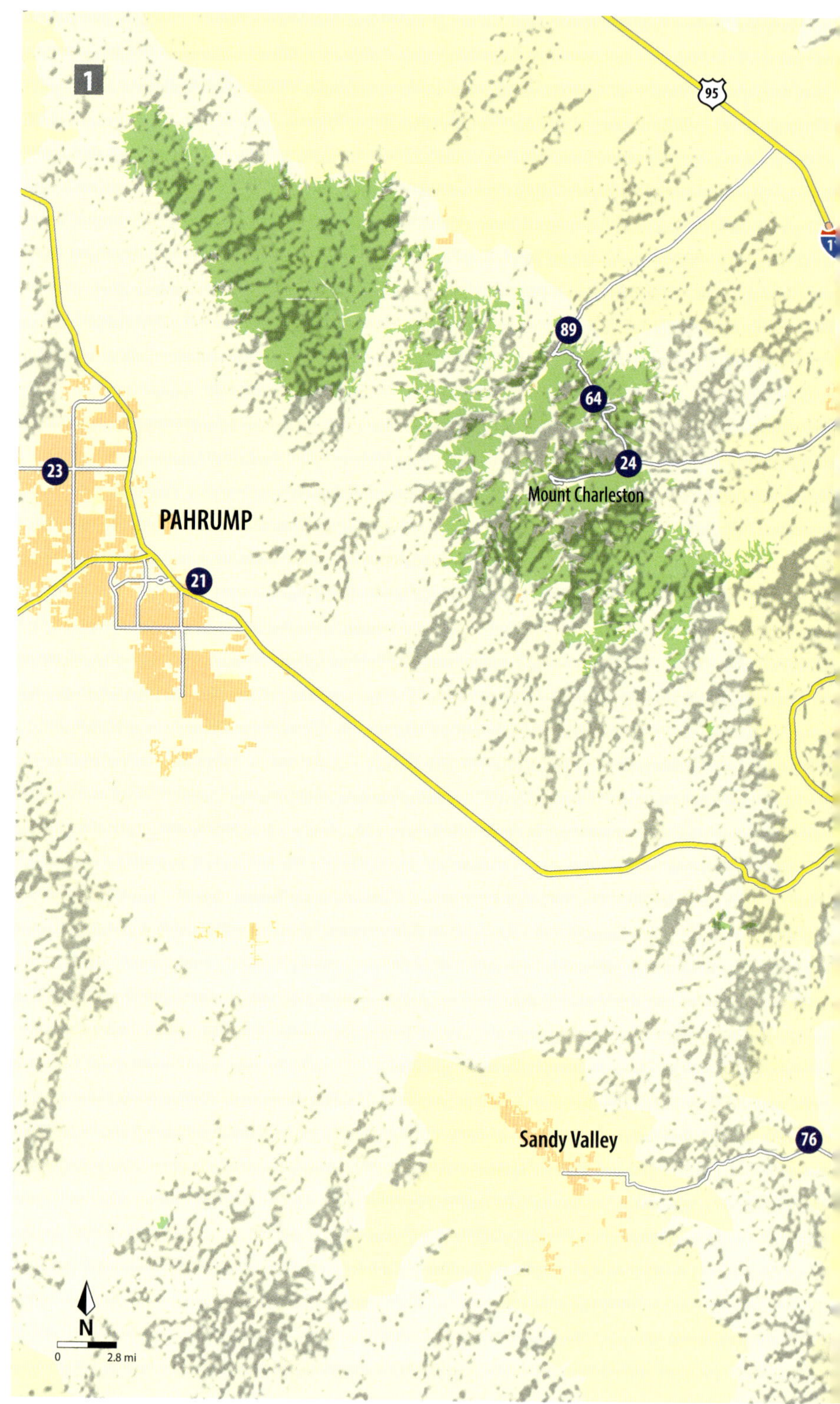
1
95
1
89
64
24
Mount Charleston
23
PAHRUMP
21
Sandy Valley
76
N
0
2.8 mi

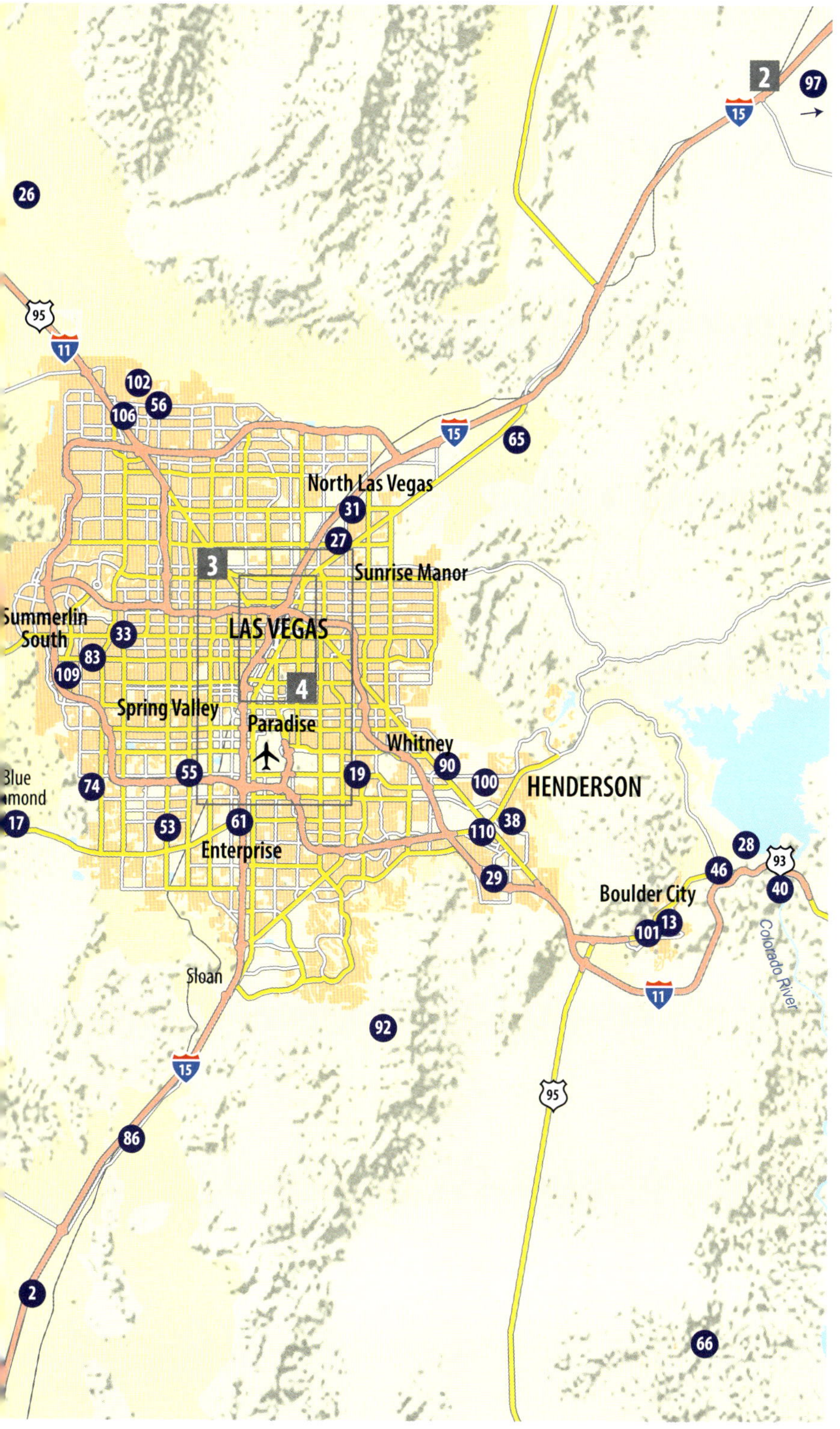

2
97
15
26
95
11
102
56
106
15
65
North Las Vegas
31
27
3
Sunrise Manor
Summerlin
South
33
LAS VEGAS
83
109
4
Spring Valley
Paradise
Whitney
Blue
mond
55
74
19
90
100
HENDERSON
17
53
61
Enterprise
110
38
28
93
46
29
Boulder City
40
13
101
Colorado River
Sloan
11
92
15
95
86
2
66

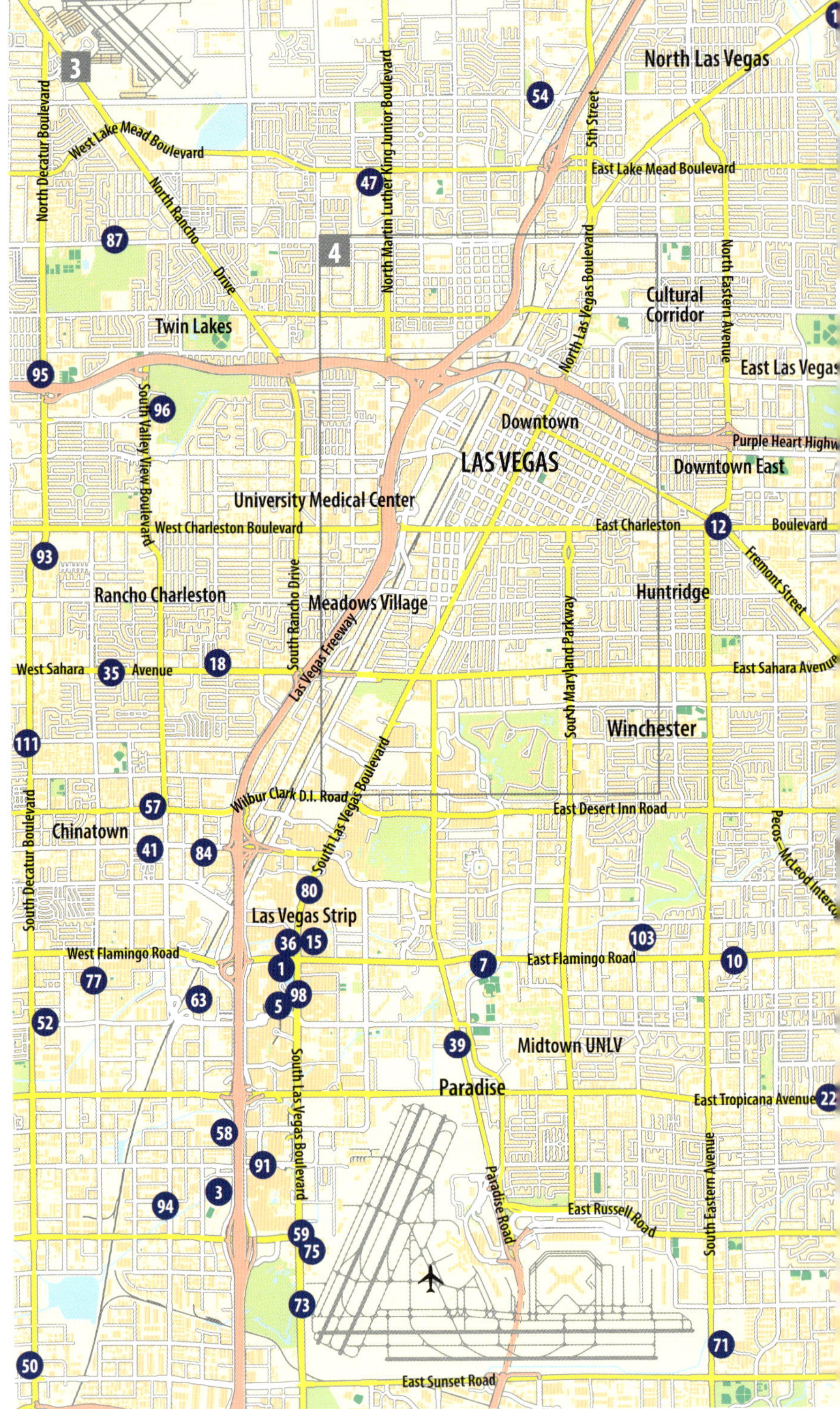

North Las Vegas
West Lake Mead Boulevard
East Lake Mead Boulevard
North Decatur Boulevard
North Rancho Drive
North Martin Luther King Junior Boulevard
5th Street
North Las Vegas Boulevard
North Eastern Avenue
Cultural Corridor
Twin Lakes
East Las Vegas
South Valley View Boulevard
Downtown
LAS VEGAS
Purple Heart Highw
Downtown East
University Medical Center
West Charleston Boulevard
East Charleston
Boulevard
Fremont Street
Rancho Charleston
Meadows Village
Huntridge
South Rancho Drive
Las Vegas Freeway
South Maryland Parkway
West Sahara
Avenue
East Sahara Avenue
Winchester
Wilbur Clark D.I. Road
South Las Vegas Boulevard
East Desert Inn Road
Pecos-McLeod Interco
Chinatown
South Decatur Boulevard
Las Vegas Strip
West Flamingo Road
East Flamingo Road
Midtown UNLV
Paradise
East Tropicana Avenue
Paradise Road
East Russell Road
South Eastern Avenue
East Sunset Road

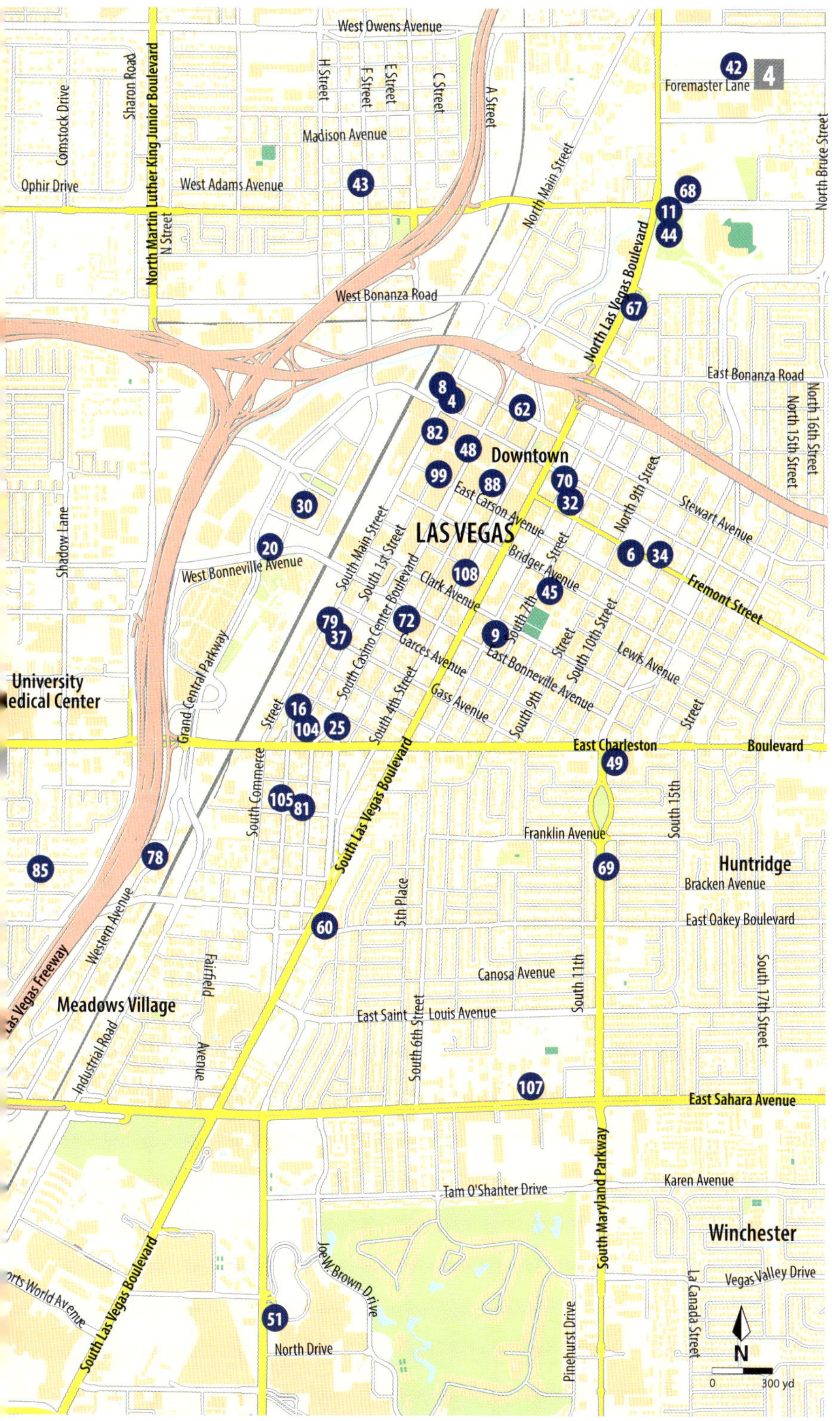
4
West Owens Avenue
H Street
F Street
E Street
C Street
A Street
Madison Avenue
West Adams Avenue
Comstock Drive
Sharon Road
Ophir Drive
North Martin Luther King Junior Boulevard
N Street
North Main Street
Foremaster Lane
North Bruce Street
North Las Vegas Boulevard
West Bonanza Road
East Bonanza Road
North 16th Street
North 15th Street
Downtown
LAS VEGAS
East Carson Avenue
North 9th Street
Stewart Avenue
Fremont Street
Bridger Avenue
South 7th Street
West Bonneville Avenue
Shadow Lane
South Main Street
South 1st Street
South Casino Center Boulevard
Clark Avenue
Garces Avenue
East Bonneville Avenue
South 10th Street
Lewis Avenue
Gass Avenue
South 4th Street
South 9th
Street
University
Medical Center
Grand Central Parkway
South Commerce Street
East Charleston Boulevard
South 15th
Franklin Avenue
Huntridge
Bracken Avenue
East Oakey Boulevard
South Las Vegas Boulevard
5th Place
Western Avenue
Fairfield Avenue
Canosa Avenue
South 11th
South 17th Street
Las Vegas Freeway
Meadows Village
East Saint Louis Avenue
South 6th Street
Industrial Road
East Sahara Avenue
Karen Avenue
Tam O'Shanter Drive
South Maryland Parkway
Winchester
Vegas Valley Drive
Joe W. Brown Drive
Sports World Avenue
La Canada Street
Pinehurst Drive
North Drive
N
0
300 yd
42 68 11 44 43 67 8 4 62 82 48 99 88 70 32 30 20 6 34 108 45 79 37 72 9 16 104 25 49 105 81 78 85 69 60 107 51

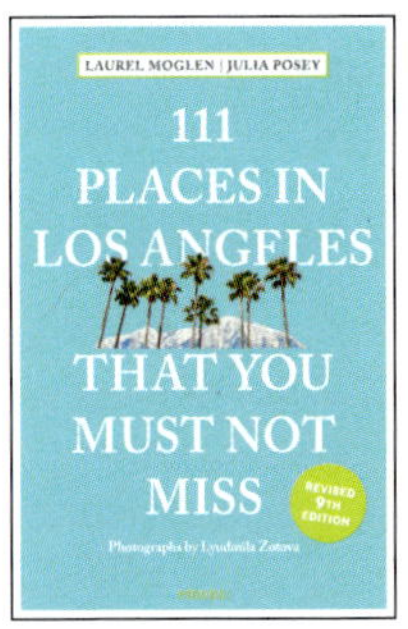

Laurel Moglen, Julia Posey, Lyudmila Zotova
111 Places in Los Angeles That You Must Not Miss
ISBN 978-3-7408-2573-7

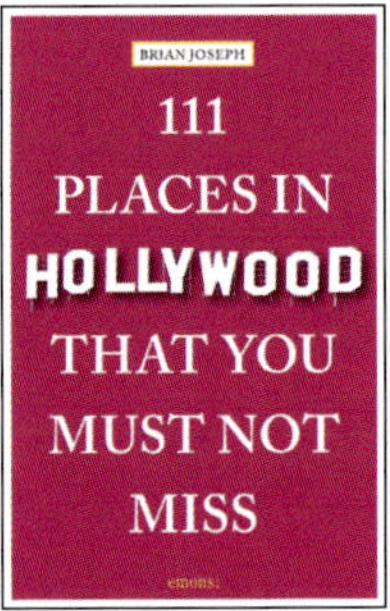

Brian Joseph
111 Places in Hollywood That You Must Not Miss
ISBN 978-3-7408-1819-7

Stephanie Arsenault
111 Places in San Diego That You Must Not Miss
ISBN 978-3-7408-1540-0

Floriana Petersen, Steve Werney
111 Places in San Francisco That You Must Not Miss
ISBN 978-3-7408-2058-9

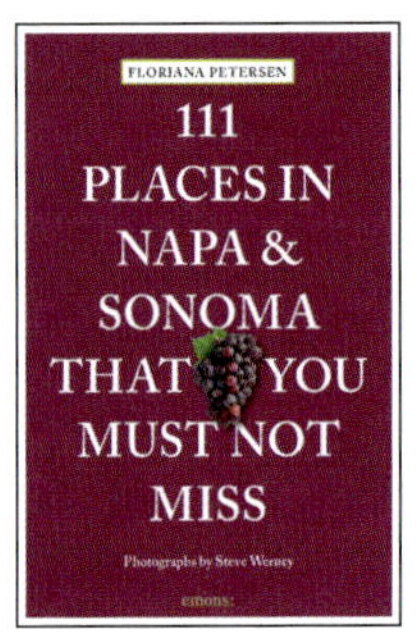

Floriana Petersen, Steve Werney
111 Places in Napa and Sonoma That You Must Not Miss
ISBN 978-3-7408-1553-0

Floriana Petersen, Steve Werney
111 Places in Silicon Valley That You Must Not Miss
ISBN 978-3-7408-1346-8

Travis Swann Taylor
111 Places in Phoenix That You Must Not Miss
ISBN 978-3-7408-2050-3

Philip D. Armour, Susie Inverso
111 Places in Denver That You Must Not Miss
ISBN 978-3-7408-1220-1

Dana DuTerroil, Joni Fincham, Daniel Jackson
111 Places in Houston That You Must Not Miss
ISBN 978-3-7408-2265-1

Dana DuTerroil, Joni Fincham, Sara S. Murphy
111 Places for Kids in Houston That You Must Not Miss
ISBN 978-3-7408-2267-5

Kelsey Roslin, Nic Yeager, Jesse Pitzler
111 Places in Austin That You Must Not Miss
ISBN 978-3-7408-1642-1

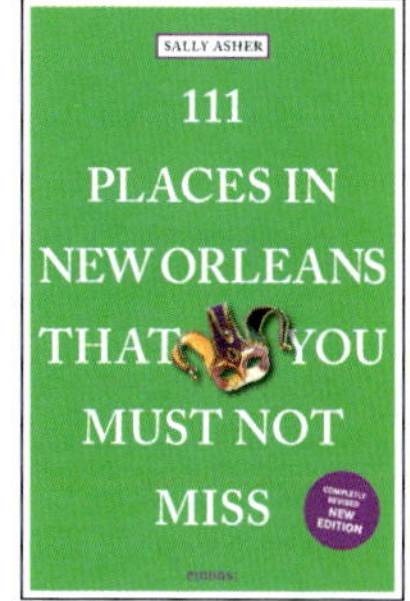

Sally Asher
111 Places in New Orleans That You Must Not Miss
ISBN 978-3-7408-2350-4

Travis Swann Taylor
111 Places in Atlanta That You Must Not Miss
ISBN 978-3-7408-1887-6

Gordon Streisand, Alex Streisand
111 Places in Miami and the Keys That You Must Not Miss
ISBN 978-3-7408-2403-7

Susan Veness, Simon Veness, Kayla Smith
111 Places in Orlando That You Must Not Miss
ISBN 978-3-7408-1900-2

Cristyle Egitto, Jakob Takos
111 Places in Palm Beach That You Must Not Miss
ISBN 978-3-7408-2398-6

John Tucker, Ashley Tucker
111 Places in Richmond That You Must Not Miss
ISBN 978-3-7408-2653-6

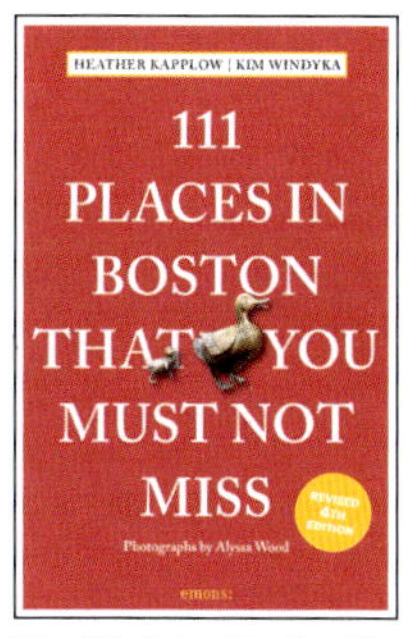

Kim Windyka, Heather Kapplow, Alyssa Wood
111 Places in Boston That You Must Not Miss
ISBN 978-3-7408-2655-0

Jo-Anne Elikann, Susan Lusk
111 Places in New York That You Must Not Miss
ISBN 978-3-7408-2400-6

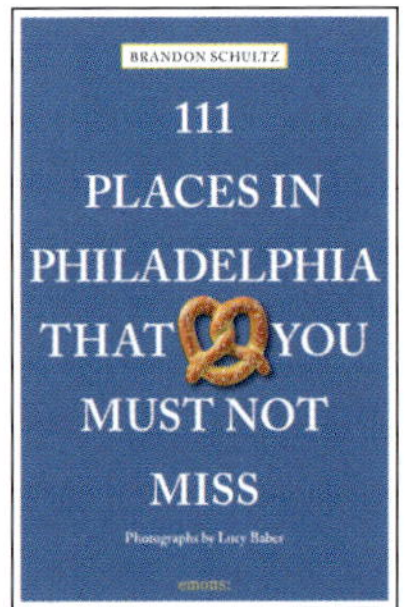

Brandon Schultz, Lucy Baber
111 Places in Philadelphia That You Must Not Miss
ISBN 978-3-7408-1376-5

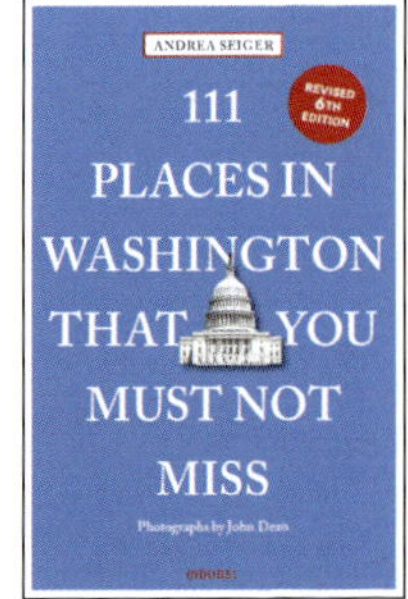

Andrea Seiger, John Dean
111 Places in Washington That You Must Not Miss
ISBN 978-3-7408-2656-7

Paige Muller, Andrea Seiger, Shedrick Pelt
22 Walks in Washington, DC That You Must Not Miss
ISBN 978-3-7408-1987-3

Lauri Williamson, David Wardrick
111 Places in Black Culture in Washington, DC That You Must Not Miss
ISBN 978-3-7408-2003-9

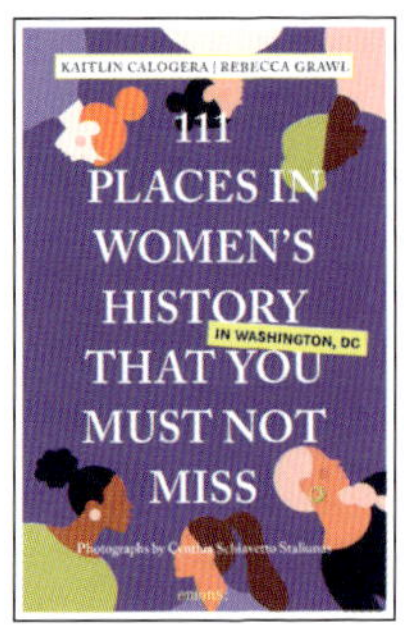

Kaitlin Calogera, Rebecca Grawl, Cynthia Schiavetto Staliunas
111 Places in Women's History in Washington That You Must Not Miss
ISBN 978-3-7408-1590-5

Amy Bizzarri, Susie Inverso
111 Places in Chicago That You Must Not Miss
ISBN 978-3-7408-2402-0

Michelle Madden, Janet McMillan
111 Places in Milwaukee That You Must Not Miss
ISBN 978-3-7408-1643-8

Elizabeth Foy Larsen
111 Places in the Twin Cities That You Must Not Miss
ISBN 978-3-7408-1347-5

Acknowledgements

This book would not have been possible without the support, encouragement, and contributions of many incredible people. I am profoundly grateful to my husband, Stephen, for reading every word, tagging along whenever possible, and for the constant pep talks while this book came together. To my kids, Andrew and Amelia, for visiting many of the locations, giving me hundreds of ideas for what to include, and for being my biggest cheerleaders.

To Kaitlyn, thank you for sharing the journey with me and experiencing some crazy and wonderful places together. My sincere thanks to Frankie Lewis for your enthusiasm and immense help in connecting us with countless members of the community. To Joe Weber, whose book *Mapping Historical Las Vegas: A Cartographic Journey* was an immense inspiration and help when trying to narrow down historic places. To Brian "Paco" Álvarez for his support and knowledge of the city's art scene.

I am incredibly thankful to my editor, Tania, for stepping in with clarity and vision, helping to shape and refine this book into what it ultimately became.

Finally, I extend my heartfelt gratitude to everyone I met in and around Las Vegas who took the time to share their stories, memories, and love for their city. This book is as much yours as it is mine.

Mackenzie Jervis is a travel writer with a background in creative writing. After exploring over 65 countries on six continents, she's found a love for uncovering the hidden stories and unique cultural gems that make each location special. After living in Vegas, she hopes to share some of what she found with longtime locals, new transplants, and frequent visitors to offer a new understanding of this energetic city.

Kaitlyn Kelsey moved from a small town in Western New York to the great city of Las Vegas in 2014 on a dare with her best friend and has been enjoying exploring the city ever since. Project manager by day and photographer by nights and weekends, you can always find her scouting for new photo locations and more often than not with a disco ball in her car and a coffee in hand. Kaitlyn has two dogs, Diesel and Missy, a love for fresh flowers, and a thirst for adventure and travel.

The information in this book was accurate at the time of publication, but it may change at any time. Please confirm the details for the places you're planning to visit before you head out on your adventures.